Thanks for the Memory

Thanks for the Memory

Ann Oughton

The Pentland Press Limited
Edinburgh • Cambridge • Durham

© Ann Oughton 1995

First published in 1995 by
The Pentland Press Ltd.
1 Hutton Close
South Church
Bishop Auckland
Durham

British Library Cataloguing in Publication Data.
A catalogue record for this book is available
from the British Library.

ISBN 1 85821 261 8

Typeset by CBS, Felixstowe, Suffolk
Printed and bound by Antony Rowe Ltd., Chippenham

For Vettinia

CONTENTS

LIST OF ILLUSTRATIONS

Most of the pictures are from the collection of Julian Twiston Davies, nephew of Don Ross. Although every effort has been made to ascertain the owners of copyright it has not always been possible to trace them and apologies are offered for any inadvertent infringement.

ACKNOWLEDGEMENTS

I would like to thank the following:

Julian Twiston Davies, without whose help and co-operation this book would not have been possible.

Max Tyler, Historian of the B.M.H.S. 'Leicester Mercury' for allowing me to reproduce the photograph of Don Ross beside his wife's portrait in the former Gaiety Theatre, South Wigston, also for their permission to refer to various excerpts from newspaper reports from their files.

Edinburgh Evening News.

FOREWORD

I love music hall. I love its songs, comic and sentimental, its jokes, squeaky clean and honestly vulgar and, most of all, its people, big, small, beautiful, gross, honest or dodgy. They are all in this fitting tribute to two of music hall's most endearing personalities. The petite, silver-voiced Gertie Gitana and her husband, the urbane, immaculate showman Don Ross.

Gertie, alas, I only saw from a seat in the gallery at the Croydon Empire but Don, after Gertie's death, became a friend and a great influence. Music hall has become, via the radio producer Charles Chilton and others too numerous to mention here, an important and wonderful part of my life. No one played a bigger part in that than Mr Ross.

Don was the first President of the British Music Hall Society. They couldn't have had a better one. He, like me, loved everything about that vanished red plush and gilt world and I was thrilled and honoured when he invited me to speak at one of their early meetings. His invitation was no printed circular. It was a handwritten card *and* contained an invitation to lunch at Simpsons. Of course I went. Me, at Simpsons! Me, who'd never eaten at a place where the ashtrays didn't have 'Newcastle Brown' stamped on them! Me, sharing a meal with the man who'd barnstormed all around Britain with the show that made me want to go into the business, 'Thanks For The Memory'. The lunch was polite, businesslike and very enjoyable. I agreed to talk to the Society, did, and thought that was that. The following summer I was in Yarmouth and the then 'Mr Yarmouth' Jack Jay invited me to an after-the-show supper at his home. Just myself, his missus Freda and a special guest – Don. Freda had made a 'music hall supper' – what else? – boiled beef and carrots. Over the coffee I asked Don a thousand questions. He answered them all with the patience of a much-loved uncle. He warmed to his subject. He told delicious tales of naughtiness in the theatre and then he started to quote songs. He sang, softly, ballads, point numbers, comic ones (both clean and Rabelaisian) and, best of all, Gertie's songs. 'Silver Bell', 'When I Leave The World Behind' and, in a style far removed from the 'chucking out time' versions I was used to, 'Nellie Dean'. Don made the song sweet, touching, *and* he told its story. 'That was how she did it,' he said, 'with love.' I suddenly knew just how insidious and compelling the best music-hall songs really are. That never-to-be-forgotten evening changed my whole view of so-called 'cheap music'. Of course I asked Don to substantiate the legendary tale of Gertie in pantomime. Left alone in the kitchen, (Buttons, her father and her two sisters having gone to the Ball) 'Cinderella' weeps for a while then declares 'Here I sit all alone, I think I'll play my saxophone!'. Reaching up the chimney our heroine pulls down the said instrument and snappily goes into the act! 'Did it ever happen?' I asked. The great man chuckled and (did I detect a blush?) replied 'You'll never know.' Rotter!

There were many unasked questions that night but Ann Oughton has almost read my mind and, in *Thanks For The Memory*, has answered them for me. Gertie's amazing childhood beginnings. Her relationship with Belle O'Connor. Her meeting Don. His strange courtship of her. His introduction to management, his adventures with the Royal Imperial Circus and his record-breaking idea for the 'Thanks For The Memory' stage show. It's all here. The story Ann has to tell is a fascinating one to those of us who care about show business. But it is much more than a list of anecdotes, dates and places. It is a love story. The popular female top of the bill starved of romance taking up with her toy boy? Well, that's what we're all led to believe but, as their story unfolds, you begin to realise that this was no ordinary, predictable hitching oneself to a great lady's wagon. They were both grafters. Gertie a painstaking perfectionist and Don, via his punishing years as a dancer, a man who aimed for taste and class in everything he produced. His kindness and concern for his wife, and hers for him, shines out from every page. When one was suffering the other was always there to comfort and guide. The description of their final parting I defy anyone to read with a dry eye. Of course Don carried on to become King Rat of The Grand Order of Water Rats, founded the British Music Hall Society and introduced me, and many others, to the magic of the halls but somehow, without his beloved Gertie, you always felt he was just marking time till they could be together again. Now they are and, I have no doubt, are looking down with an arm round each other's shoulder thinking 'No one will ever know if the "Cinderella" story is true or not'. Dear Don, dear Gertie and Ann Oughton – thanks for the memory.

Roy Hudd,
President of the British Music Hall Society.
1995.

CHAPTER 1

LITTLE GITANA

When Lavinia Agnes Kilkenny and William Astbury married on 10th October 1886 at St Luke's church in Hanley, they could never have suspected that their first-born child was destined to become one of music hall's shining stars, the first Forces' sweetheart, or that she would be granted the honour of having a street named after her.

It was on 28th December 1887 that Gertrude Mary Astbury made her very first appearance in a humble dwelling at number 7, Shirley Street, Longport. It was the year of Queen Victoria's Golden Jubilee, Merry Hampton had won the Derby and that greatest of all fictional detectives, Sherlock Holmes, made his debut along with Dr Watson in Conan Doyle's *A Study in Scarlet*.

When Vinnie had to give up her job as a schoolteacher in order to care for their baby, the Astburys' income was severely depleted. The little family moved to Burslem when Gertie was six weeks old and Vinnie managed a general store in order to eke out William's meagre pay of thirty shillings a week as a pottery worker. They settled there quite happily and the following year the family welcomed the birth of a son, whom they christened James.

As soon as Gertie was able to walk she was entertaining. She loved to play with her dolls who comprised her very first audience. When the weather was fine she would sit them in line on the windowsill outside her mother's shop and demonstrate a little singing and dancing. The dolls were not the only ones to be amused, passers-by would often stop to watch and applaud the pretty dancer. It had began as a device to occupy herself whilst her mother was kept busy running the shop, but it was evident to all who saw her that the little girl was a born

1

performer.

It was during one of these sessions that two girls from Tomkinson's Royal Gypsy Children's Troupe saw Gertie dancing in the street. Like the other passers-by, they found her quite delightful to watch and they stopped to play with her. They taught her some of the steps from their own dancing routine as well as skipping with a rope and clog dancing, which was the precursor of modern tap dancing.

The Gypsy Troupe was very popular in the Potteries towns, as well as in Wales, and Tom Tomkinson would take his juvenile performers on tour of the local halls in a horse-drawn wagonette.

Minstrel groups with their cork-blackened faces had been in vogue for some time. The Livermore Brothers had blazed a trail along which followed Sam Haigh, Moore and Burgess and Haverley's Minstrels, who had provided the vehicle for Eugene Stratton to find fame in England. He was so adept at the soft-shoe dancing that all who saw him on stage swore that his feet hardly touched the floor. But Tom Tomkinson gave the audiences something new with his little group of juvenile performers, with their all-white faces and a completely different style of dance.

Gertie loved playing with her new-found friends and she pleaded with them to allow her to join in their dancing with the Troupe. They agreed to take her along to one of their rehearsals at the Welsh Chapel in Burslem on the understanding that she must sit quietly at the back of the hall and not get in the way. Gertie could hardly contain her excitement as she hopped and skipped along with the older girls all the way to the Chapel.

Rehearsals were only just underway when Mr Tomkinson noticed one little girl at the back of the hall who simply could not sit still. As the other children went through their routines she would join in and copy their actions. He watched her and was amazed at the ease with which she mastered the most intricate steps without any prompting. There was no precocity about her and yet she displayed the confidence and poise redolent of a true professional. Tom Tomkinson also discovered that this little girl had a unique singing voice. It was clear and tuneful with a maturity far in advance of her years.

He knew star material when he saw it, the child was 'a natural' and he wasted no time in contacting Gertie's mother to seek permission for her little daughter to join his Troupe. Permission was granted and at the tender age of four Gertie was on the road, travelling with the company around the halls in the Potteries. She was the brightest, prettiest little person in the Troupe and by the time she was six she was topping the bill as 'Little Gitana'.

Gitana is the Italian feminine for gypsy and the little girl, with her thick dark tresses, brilliant blue eyes and diminutive physique certainly could have been taken for a gypsy child. She was striking in appearance and, although small in stature, her presence filled not only the stage but the entire hall.

Little Gitana

As well as one-night stands in the Potteries the Troupe began to venture farther afield and for longer periods, but it was not until they had stopped for a week in Eastbourne that Vinnie had an opportunity to see her daughter perform on stage. No doubt she was also looking forward to the rare treat of an outing but, when Vinnie arrived at the theatre and saw how Gertie had been billed, she was furious and Mr Tomkinson experienced the sharp edge of Vinnie's tongue.

SPECIAL ENGAGEMENT at ENORMOUS EXPENSE
of
ENGLAND'S PREMIER MIDGET COMEDIENNE
WONDERFUL LITTLE GITANA
The unapproachable Lilliputian Song
and Dance Artiste. Tyrolean Yodeller
Male Impersonator and Paper Tearer.

Vinnie could hardly contain her anger when she saw her daughter advertised as a midget, as if she were 'Some sort of freak'. She insisted that the bill matter be changed immediately or she would take Gertie home with her that instant. Of course, Tom Tomkinson wanted to retain his child star so he complied with Vinnie's wishes, the words 'midget' and 'Lilliputian' were hastily erased from the notices and Gertie was allowed to remain with the Troupe.

When on tour there were two wardrobe mistresses who kept a motherly eye on the girls and Tom Tomkinson kept the boys in check. His brother, Arthur, was the advance man, always going on ahead to organise their accommodation and the advertising of the show. They travelled through the Welsh valleys and wherever they appeared everyone marvelled at the 'Little Gitana'. Gertie was not only a good performer, she possessed a natural charm and grace as well as a certain quality which can only be described as magic. She truly enchanted all who saw her. Even at this tender age and tiny as she was, Gertie was able to attract attention. Her neat appearance and dainty mannerisms meant that she only had to walk on stage to receive rapturous applause and she certainly enjoyed the limelight. From the very beginning she had that special gift, the ability to establish an instant rapport with any audience.

Sadly, it was during their tour of the Welsh valleys that tragedy befell the little Troupe. They were playing Merthyr Tydfil when Tom Tomkinson became ill. He contracted pneumonia, which was said to have been brought on by his having slept in too many cold and damp lodgings. Whatever the cause, he died and Tomkinson's Gypsy Troupe returned to Hanley.

Tom's brother, Arthur, took over the management of the Troupe and he demonstrated true entrepreneurial skill when he devised an entirely new format for the show before resuming the tour. Although the dancers were to remain in the first part of the show, the second half was to be devoted to variety. As these acts were always engaged on a weekly basis there was a constant turnover, but, like his brother, he realised the potential drawing power of having a good act at the top of the bill and so a permanent spot was always reserved for their star turn, 'Little Gitana'. A finale was written especially for her, a musical comedy entitled *Marita, Queen of the Romany*. It was designed to highlight all Gertie's talents.

The new show brought in excellent business and played to full houses seven days a week. The Sabbath was kept holy by putting on a 'Grand Sacred Concert', which included hymn singing interspersed by readings from the Bible and a book entitled *Only a Gypsy*. There were magic lantern slides and all to the accompaniment of a full orchestra. Although the success of this grand production meant their working every day of the week, the children did not mind in the least. They regarded it as play, indeed if there had been ten days in a week they would have gladly worked every single one.

After a successful tour with the new format the Gypsy Troupe returned to their home base in Hanley for the summer holidays. Gertie was delighted to be back with her parents. She had a new baby brother now and she spent most of her time tending to and playing with him.

Although it had been an accidental process, Gertie had already found success as a performer. She had talent, there could be no doubt about that, but she had also shown that she possessed the essential stamina and perseverance necessary for a life of touring in variety. The fact that she also had personal charm and was able to get along well with her peers was evident. She had been singled out, made the star of this little show, a career move that might have caused friction, even jealousy among the other older members of the Troupe. In fact, one would have expected some animosity but there was never the slightest suggestion of ill-feeling ever between Gertie and her fellow performers. Throughout her life, on stage or off, she was loved and admired by all who knew her. It was impossible to dislike Gertie.

Talent is an essential factor for any artiste but all the charm and talent in the world is never quite enough on its own. In order to achieve stardom a little luck is necessary and Gertie's stroke of luck appeared in the guise of Mrs Belle O'Connor.

Vinnie showed Mrs O'Connor into the parlour, that inner sanctum of the working class home. Although smartly dressed, a little too smart for Vinnie's liking, and she was wearing make-up, Vinnie refused to be impressed by her uninvited guest and we can almost hear her tut-tutting her disapproval as she offered Mrs O'Connor a cup of tea. At least she was prepared to listen to what Mrs O'Connor had to say. 'My husband, Jimmy O'Connor, and I run a show in music halls round the country. We are in Barrow-in-Furness this week and we first heard about your little girl from one of our artistes who saw her perform. We would like her to join us.' There was no reply from Vinnie. No doubt she was still trying to size up her unexpected visitor.

Vinnie was a strong-willed woman, accustomed to making all the family decisions and accustomed to getting her own way. Mrs O'Connor's smart clothes and make-up might be all right in the world of the theatre, but here in the Potteries . . .

Mrs O'Connor was also a woman of determination, she usually got her own way too and she continued, 'If your little girl came with us she would be well looked after and the experience she would gain from appearing in just one of our shows . . . Well, suffice to say we would ensure that she was groomed for stardom.'

Vinnie broke her silence, 'Mrs O'Connor, our girl is barely eight years old. I don't know if it would be right for her to go on the stage, not permanently. The Gypsy Troupe was all right, for a while . . .'

Mrs O'Connor persisted, 'Mrs Astbury, I have assured you that your child's welfare will be our first priority. From what I've been told she has the potential to be a great star.'

Vinnie still hesitated. Belle O'Connor made to leave and shot her parting bolt,

'Just think, Mrs Astbury, in years to come your daughter might never forgive you for not allowing her to seize this chance.'

Without making any promises Vinnie agreed to discuss the matter with her husband when he returned from work.

Belle smiled to herself. 'I will arrange to stay overnight and return here at ten in the morning. There's a train leaving for Barrow at noon. If you decide to let your girl come with us please have her packed up and ready to leave on that midday train.' Having delivered her ultimatum, Belle O'Connor left.

Vinnie's thoughts were in turmoil as Belle O'Connor's words echoed through her mind. How could she stand in the way of her daughter's future success and yet how could she, a caring mother, allow her child to be taken from home by total strangers. Not only strangers but theatrical people at that. No matter how well they might care for her, Gertie was bound to be influenced by their peculiar life style.

For once in her life, Vinnie was at a loss. She could not make this decision alone. A staunch Catholic, her first resort was the local priest, after which she went to see Arthur Tomkinson. We do not know what the priest's recommendation was but Tomkinson assured Vinnie that this was indeed an opportunity that should not be passed up. Although he did not want to lose his star performer, he reminded Vinnie that her daughter might never get another chance like it.

The atmosphere in the Astbury household must have been fraught that evening as Vinnie explained Belle O'Connor's proposal. William was fervently opposed to the idea. He did not want to see his only daughter leave home. She was far too young and her time with the Gypsy Troupe had been child's play, a source of amusement, nothing more. As for the music hall and all the talk of making it a career, that was something entirely different and he would have none of it.

The final decision, as always, was made by Vinnie, and she must have already reached that decision before the family discussion took place, even before she realised it herself. They could have talked all night without reaching a consensus. Quietly, she began to collect Gertie's things together.

Gertie did not want to leave home for an unknown destination. There were tears, floods of them as she watched her mother pack her belongings in the little rush portmanteau and she pleaded with Vinnie not to send her away. Nothing that

Vinnie could say would convince Gertie that this move was for her own benefit. Her big chance. Finally Vinnie placated her by promising that if she would only give it a trial for two weeks she could return home if she was still unhappy. She was not being abandoned. They would keep in touch and, if necessary, Vinnie would come and collect her.

Gertie dried her tears and soon after ten the next morning, as arranged, she obediently turned her back on the little Potteries town that had been her home for her first eight years. We can only imagine Vinnie's mixed feelings as she waved farewell and entrusted the care of her only daughter to a stranger. Belle O'Connor must have been reminded of how she had first set out on her own career as she led the little girl away.

Belle had been much older than Gertie, all of fifteen, when her parents had reluctantly given their permission for her to tour with Mr and Mrs Brogdon's Refined Swiss Choir. Her original name had been Mabel Walker. Her father was a successful Leicestershire businessman and her mother a rather straight-laced Victorian lady. Belle had been taught dancing and singing at school and adopted her grandmother's surname, calling herself Belle Houghton, when she embarked upon her stage career. She was twenty-one and on her way to engagements in Ireland when she met and fell in love with Jimmy O'Connor.

Jimmy, born Wignall, came from Bradford and had started his stage career by performing at church concerts and public houses after his working day at a butcher's cash desk was finished. He formed a partnership with Charlie Brady and their act was billed as the 'Music Hall Butchers'. Jim inherited the name O'Connor from Brady's previous partner.

Belle's mother was opposed to her marrying Jimmy so they married quietly in a registry office within a year of their meeting. After a working honeymoon on the continent they returned to Britain, where Jimmy set up his own business organising and producing his own shows.

Belle and Jimmy looked after their young charge well and wrote to Vinnie and William that Gertie had settled with them and was happy. Her starting salary was to be three pounds a week. One pound would be sent to Vinnie, five shillings was Gertie's own pocket money and the remaining thirty-five shillings would be used to pay for her board and lodgings, travelling expenses and the provision of her stage costumes. It was a fair arrangement and everyone was happy with it.

When, after the two weeks' trial period, Gertie was asked if she wanted to stay with the O'Connors or return to Hanley she replied, after a little thought, 'I'll give it another week.'

The other week came and went and there was never any question of Gertie leaving the O'Connors. Auntie Belle and Uncle Jimmy soon became as close to Gertie as her own parents had been. In many ways they were perhaps closer, certainly the care and love they bestowed upon her were as much as might be expected from the most devoted of parents. What had started as a business partnership soon developed into a close personal relationship that was to last for the entirety of Gertie's life.

Gertie's first appearance as a single solo performer was at the Tivoli Theatre soon after her arrival in Barrow. It was customary for music hall performers to stand in the wings and watch the other artistes go through their routine but on this particular night, before the show started, Jimmy O'Connor called them all together. 'I'm putting the kid on tonight and I want you all to stay in your dressing rooms. She's bound to be nervous and I don't want any distractions.'

Jimmy need not have worried. Confidently, Gertie made her entrance and sang three songs. All went well until she left the stage. The audience would not stop applauding. Jimmy shooed her back, 'Give them another song. Quick.' Gertie did not know what to do next. 'I don't know any more songs.' It was Jimmy O'Connor's turn to feel lost. 'Well, you've got to do something, anything!' Gertie rose to the occasion; returning to the stage she whispered to the conductor of the orchestra, 'Please, Mr Conductor, can you play the hornpipe?'

Gertie finished her act with her little hornpipe dance to further extended applause. If he had not realised it before, he certainly knew it now: Jimmy O'Connor had a star on his hands.

That was only the first of many successes and the life and ways of the music hall soon became routine for Gertie. Although she may well have been just a little homesick at first, it could not last because there was so much going on around her. The new world in which she found herself was fascinating and she loved the travel and diversity of places and people which it offered. There was no shortage of playmates. The children of the family acts were ever present to befriend and amuse. Gertie loved animals and there were many animal acts which were popular with the audiences of the day, such as Harry Rochez's Monkey Music Hall. His sister Doria had a dog act entitled 'In the Maid's Absence', in which the dogs performed a scene acting as the lady's maids. Madame Dalmere had performing monkeys, dogs, cats, rats and two large Amazonian parrots and she would never allow bad language to be used in front of her animals.

All in all, Gertie enjoyed a happy, carefree childhood. What she did on stage she never regarded as being 'work', far from it, she loved every minute she spent before the footlights. She was certainly well cared for by Auntie and Uncle O'Connor and always enjoyed the luxury of her own private dressing room wherever she appeared. The law decreed that no child performer should share a dressing room with an adult. With Belle and Jimmy to manage her career and her life, Gertie was able to channel all her energies into entrancing her ever increasing audiences.

One incident illustrates just how well the O'Connors looked after Gertie's best interests. It was in 1900 that Jimmy had booked a date for Gertie at the Bedford Music Hall in London. It looked as if it could be a good opportunity for her, she would be in the mainstream at last. It was just a few minutes before she was due on stage when Belle was informed that Gertie had been billed to go on first. Furious with the management she took her protegée by the hand and marched out of the theatre.

The first spot on the programme was the worst possible placing for any artiste. Most of the audience would still be arriving, calling across the hall to friends, chattering to each other and generally making a din, but worst of all, the last thing they would be doing would be paying any attention to the act on stage.

Jim complained, 'This child is no beginner. She deserves a better placing. She would be wasted on an inattentive audience when half of them are still arriving, chattering to each other and banging down their seats. Four years of hard graft in the provinces could go down the drain because of bad placing.'

The theatre management responded with the offer of a better spot on the programme.

LITTLE GITANA
A vocalist with a wonderful voice
An actress second to none
A dancer equal to any
Must be seen and heard to be believed

Such was the advert placed by a jubilant Jimmy O'Connor in the professional paper *The Era* when that first engagement in London led to six further bookings at the Bedford. In fact, everyone who saw Gertie perform wanted her and demands for contracts were already flooding in from agents. Soon she was working three halls a night and her weekly entry in *The Era* in January 1901 was as follows:

LITTLE GITANA
Brixton Empress 8.35 p.m.
Royal Holborn 9.30 p.m.
Collins Music Hall 10.20 p.m.

At that time performances in most theatres were restricted to once nightly and there was no law regulating children's appearances on stage, so it was possible indeed customary for a minor to work the same hours as an adult performer. The only legal requirement regarding children was that a licence had to be obtained from the magistrates of the town in which the child was appearing. Of course the O'Connors were always meticulous in following such regulations.

It does seem hard by today's standards that a child should be working such late hours, beginning a final performance at 10.20 at night. This was at the turn of the century and many children from similar backgrounds to Gertie were forced to work in factories in abysmal conditions for very little remuneration; boys of Gertie's age were working in the mines. By the time she was fifteen Gertie was earning more than £100 a week, more than her father had ever earned in one single year, for doing something which delighted her.

It could not have been an easy task getting from one theatre to another in time for the next performance. It was a tight schedule and, although the traffic of

London may not have been quite as congested then as it is today, considerable distances had to be covered in a short space of time, usually by horse-drawn vehicles.

Despite her outstanding success as a charming child performer, the time was fast approaching for Gertie to grow up. This was a dangerous time for many juvenile artistes, who often disappeared from the scene because they were unable to make that difficult transition from child star to adult entertainer. The audiences of the day loved a good child performer and, because Gertie was small for her age and had always appeared younger than her years, she had been able to get away with being 'Little Gitana' for longer than most others might have managed.

Belle had an idea for a new act. She had devised it herself and entitled it 'The Schoolgirl's Holiday'. It was first produced at Gatti's Theatre, Westminster Bridge Road, on 28th December 1903, on Gertie's sixteenth birthday.

It was a 'one woman show' with Gertie presenting all the items as she re-enacted the scenes from an end of term school concert to amuse her dolls. She sang a coon song, did a schottische dance followed by a sentimental ballad or two and, finally, the characterisation of an inebriate known as 'Piccadilly Johnny'. As always when Gertie was performing, the audiences were more than enthusiastic but one press critic was unamused and stated that, although Gertie was undoubtedly a 'clever little person', he would have preferred not to see drunkenness 'so openly displayed by one so young.'

He was right. It had been a mistake to include such a personification in the act of one who was noted for her innocence and sincerity. When the people came to see Gertie Gitana they came because they knew they could be sure of seeing a good clean act which always attracted the better-class, family-type of audience.

It could be delayed no longer, the title 'Little' had to go. Although Gertie was no taller, throughout her life she remained a petite five foot in her small stockinged feet, she was no longer a child and the problem of finding an appropriate name for her had to be faced. Many names were put forward but none of them had the ring of suitability. Certainly, there were none that took Belle's fancy.

As so often happens in such situations the answer was all too obvious. So much so that Belle and Jimmy wondered that they had not thought of it before. One of the agents asked Belle, 'What is her real name?' As soon as he heard that it was Gertrude he had the solution in an instant, 'That's it, Gertie Gitana. That's two hard G's, a good alliteration. It rolls off the tongue.' It certainly did and it continued to roll off the tongue of many a fan for years to come. They had rid themselves of the 'Little' but the well-known 'Gitana' remained.

That was one problem solved but it was by no means the most difficult. If Gertie had to grow up, so did the act. She could not continue to use the same material as she had when she was 'Little Gitana'. No longer a child but the fresh innocent approach had to be retained. For her to feature the type of music hall song for which Marie Lloyd or Vesta Tilley were famous would have been inappropriate, to say the least. Although Gertie's audiences loved her and would have continued to love her no matter what she did, the choice of material for her now was to be more difficult than ever before. The childish songs had to go but the new songs must continue to promote the sentiments for which she had become famous.

Gertie

In 1905 Jimmy booked Gertie to appear for two weeks at the Lyceum in the Strand and she was one of the few artistes to succeed there during the Lyceum's brief period as a music hall under the management of Jim Barrassford. Jimmy O'Connor was a shrewd businessman and he deliberately kept her date book free beyond those two weeks. He knew Gertie and, if previous performances were anything to go by, there would be many offers from managers wishing to book her for their theatres. Big theatres with big audiences. So that when the manager of the Holborn Empire called Jimmy to say that he had a 'turn off' and was desperate for a replacement, Jimmy was able to oblige him. 'She's a young kid who's really doing well. Used to be Little Gitana but is now billed as Gertie Gitana.'

The manager of the Holburn Empire was doubtful. It was a late spot on the bill. Could the girl handle it? Jimmy assured him that she could, and she did.

Gertie made her appearance and the applause from the delighted audience almost brought the house down.

That term at the Holborn Empire lasted for two weeks which led to bookings at the Ardwick Empire, Manchester, where she topped the bill as a solo artiste for the first time. Once an artiste had reached that point in their career, they were in the enviable position of being able to name their price for subsequent appearances. Gertie Gitana was well and truly on her way.

Oswald Stoll, later to become Sir Oswald, of the Stoll Empire's group of theatres, was an impresario who recognised Gertie's potential from the first time he saw her perform. Noted for his rather puritanical nature, he never allowed any bawdiness or raucous behaviour in his theatres and it was common to see notices displayed in theatres throughout the Stoll Empire's circuit informing the audience on how to behave. There were to be no cat calls or similar vulgarity. The audience must show their appreciation by genteel hand clapping alone.

For Oswald Stoll Gertie was a gift, she was the epitome of the kind of music hall entertainment that he had worked so hard to promote. It was Oswald Stoll who was responsible for bestowing upon Gertie the titles which were destined to appear subsequently on all her bill matter, 'Idol of the People' and 'The Star Who Never Fails to Shine'. Whenever she saw or heard the latter tribute Gertie could never resist the temptation to add, 'Even without the aid of metal polish!'

Joking apart, throughout her entire career Gertie never once failed to shine. She never gave a performance that was anything less than superlative and she shone in the days before microphones or the sophisticated electronic sound systems which are in common use today. She did not need any mechanical assistance to reach every single person in the theatre.

Unlike one music hall performer who seemed to make a point of singing ever more quietly: as time went on and Maidie Scott became quieter still, the audiences were inclined to shout at her to sing up. When Gertie suggested to Maidie that the people at the back of the hall might not be able to hear her, Maidie shrugged and replied airily, 'I don't care. My work is for the stalls and the dress circle. To hell with the pit and the top shelf!'

Gertie did care. She saw it as her duty to give pleasure to every single person who had paid their hard-earned money to see and hear her.

There were many occasions when Gertie's audiences would not allow her to leave the stage and, although she was ever willing to repeat encore after encore, she also thought of her fellow artistes. After one performance, when the audience had been particularly demanding, Gertie held up her hand to halt the applause. She explained that, although she was grateful for their appreciation, there were other performers who had to earn their living too. If she did another encore their performing time would be reduced as well as their income.

When Gertie appeared for the first time at the Argyle Theatre in Birkenhead in 1904, she ran true to form and stormed the audiences. The local newspaper declared that, 'This artiste made one of the greatest hits ever known at the Argyle.'

The proprietor of the Argyle, Dennis Clarke, was known and respected for his business acumen, honesty and his insistence on a good clean show. Every Monday night first house Dennis Clarke would position himself in a box at one side of the stage and his wife would occupy the box opposite. Each would be armed with notebook and pencil and any joke or comment which they considered to be in dubious taste was duly recorded. Any comedian appearing at the Argyle would await the dreaded knock on the dressing room door after their first performance, which invariably meant that Mr and Mrs Clarke requested that they remove from their act any material which they had considered to be indelicate. It meant that the offending comic would have his work cut out to re-write his material in time for the second house performance.

Dennis Clarke was so impressed by Gertie that he approached Jimmy O'Connor with a contract for return performances with regular increments for the following ten years. Like others before him, Dennis Clarke also had a nose for talent and it was his habit to sign up young performers whom he considered to be star potential on a long-term contract. The Argyle was a truly old-time music hall which had developed from what had been originally a public house. It was compact, providing seating for only 800, and thanks to Dennis Clarke, many great names of music hall got their foot on the first rung of the ladder when they appeared at the Argyle. The long-term contract was a good business ploy as far as he was concerned and Gertie exceeded even Dennis Clarke's expectations. Although she was soon earning salaries far in excess of those which her contract with the Argyle had stipulated, she never failed to honour her obligation and she returned every year at the agreed, lower salary. In return, Mr Clarke would present her with a large bouquet at the end of the final Saturday night's performance. Attached to it would be a little bonus. A bag containing a handful of gold sovereigns.

Gertie never allowed money or prestige to spoil relationships which she had formed on her way up the ladder. Jimmy O'Connor had always advised her, 'Always tip well, Gertie. Remember, you go back to places.' Consequently, she always carried £200 in her handbag. If any money was spent during the course of the day it had to be replenished immediately, maintaining a balance of £200.

But it was not simply a matter of tipping well, throwing money around; Gertie always respected and remembered the people and the places she had known on her way up the ladder.

The Queen's Theatre, in the East End of London, had been run by the Abrahams family since 1856. Originally it was a 'Palace of Varieties and Public House', as were many of the music halls in those early days. Over the years Gertie had come to know the Abrahams family very well but after a time the theatre had become run down and no longer able to attract the audiences or afford the fees of the big names of music hall. Now and then Gertie's agent would call her, 'Mr Abrahams is asking if you will go back to the Queen's again.' For old times' sake Gertie would always reply, 'Of course. Pick a week and don't argue about the salary.'

CHAPTER 2

NELLIE DEAN

G ertie continued to give her audiences nothing but the best. She could fill any theatre in the land even before the advance notices had arrived. The mention of her name, the rumour that Gertie Gitana was to appear at a certain theatre, was enough to ensure that there would be standing room only on the opening night.

She was a very generous performer and never one to hog the limelight for herself, although she could easily have done so because everyone in that audience had come to see Gertie Gitana. It was because of her innate generosity and professional approach towards her work that other artistes always enjoyed appearing on the same bill. Ted Ray said of Gertie, 'She attracted a better class of audience, cleaner minded, family types.'

Music hall had been born out of the taverns, where largely working class audiences gathered to drown their sorrows. The variety of performers included acrobats and jugglers as well as comedians and singers. Their material had to be topical as well as original. Songs such as 'My Old Man said Follow the Van', introduced by Marie Lloyd, mirrored working class life of the day and music hall entertainment was considered by many to be rather low-class, even vulgar. Gertie's performance was different. There can be no doubt that she was absolutely unique. There had never been anyone like her before and there has never been anyone quite like her since. She had a clear voice with a purity and sweetness of tone. Like the title of one of her songs, a 'Silver Bell'. Her diction was perfect and every syllable of every single word was distinctly pronounced. The songs she sang were characteristic of her own nature, warm and sincere, echoing the perceptions and emotions that her mainly working class audiences could empathise with: sentimental ballads which provided an escape from the drabness and crushing poverty of their daily lives. For a while at least they could forget about the unpaid bills, inadequate housing and their shoeless children. Songs such as 'Silver Bell', 'Baby Rose' and 'Never Mind':

> Though your heart be full of pain, never mind,
> Though your face should lose its smile, never mind,
> For there's sunshine after rain,
> And gladness follows pain,
> You'll be happy once again, never mind.

Gertie was nothing if not versatile, she was an excellent tap dancer as well as being able to yodel very well. Yodelling the chorus of songs was fashionable at that time and many music hall singers incorporated it into their act but Gertie was the first woman in Britain to play the saxophone on stage. The instrument had recently been introduced from America where it had gained popularity in brass bands.

SAX ACT: I was very interested in your article (Look, last week) about the saxophone. It was invented by Antoine Joseph Sax, who patented it in 1845 and registered it in 1846. I first became aware of it in about 1911, when it was played by a music-hall entertainer named Gertie Gitana. — Frank Buckley, Feltham, Middlesex.

Gertie Gitana: popular player

Gertie always commanded a full stage setting for her act. The set would portray a lavishly furnished drawing room with a view of a conservatory at the rear. There was always a grand piano on stage and Gertie would make her entrance from the back of the stage. Just before reaching the footlights she would give a quick little run of tripping steps and bow to her audience. Every eye in the house was on her, even before she sang a note she had the audience in the palm of her hand and she knew it.

It was customary for her to sing two or three songs standing at the front of the stage before moving towards the grand piano, which was always draped with a deep-fringed silk shawl. As she did so she had a way of turning her back on the audience; then, after a pause, she would turn her head and look over her shoulder, giving them a kind of winsome, even flirtatious look. After donning a silk top hat, which she always wore at a rakish angle, she would pick up the saxophone, which must have been almost as tall as herself, and play a simple tune. This so intrigued her audiences that many of them wrote to ask what the unusual instrument was, they had never seen its like before.

Because she had such tiny feet her shoes had to be made especially for her. They were supplied by Polikoff's and later Freed's, little white suede pumps to go with her pretty white dresses. One observer noted that, 'Her skirts were worn rather shorter than the fashions of the day dictated.' If her skirts were short the overall effect was one of modesty. With her petite figure and raven tresses tumbling down over her shoulders she always had the appearance of a very young person, even childlike. Her small, pretty hands caught the imagination of photographers, who invariably requested that they be on show whenever she sat for formal portraits.

As her popularity increased Gertie was asked more and more for return performances, which created a pressing need for new material. One such request came from the Palace Theatre, Plymouth. It had been less than three months since Gertie had last appeared there, playing to full houses every night, and, although it was flattering to be requested to make a return appearance so quickly, it was also disconcerting because she had nothing new to offer them. Her professional approach to her work would not allow her to present the same material that she had already performed so recently and yet she had nothing that was either new or suitable.

Song writers and publishers would often approach a popular music hall singer and offer a song on a contract basis. Sometimes they would offer to sell a song outright to a performer who thought they could do something with it. Or there might be an agreement which would allow sole rights to one singer for six months or so before it was offered to anyone else. It was obviously a good way to sell a song if a struggling writer could persuade a well-known artiste to take it up and make it popular, but many song writers must have cursed the day they had sold a song outright which later became a best seller, so losing their copyright and all future income that it might have engendered.

Gertie's brother, Jim, had recently settled in America and he had discovered a song by the American songwriter Henry W. Armstrong (composer of 'Sweet Adeline'), which he thought was tailor-made for her. When Gertie first looked at the sheet music she was not impressed. The plain fact was that she did not particularly like the song and had stashed it away in a drawer where it had remained, almost forgotten, until now. Despite the fact that she had not thought much of it after the first playing, sheer desperation made her seek it out now and give it another airing.

Belle always had a great say in the choice of Gertie's material and she played it on the piano. She played it again as if trying to convince herself of some hidden potential that she had hitherto missed. 'It's a pretty little tune,' she admitted, 'but there's not much to it.' Gertie agreed, but, 'We have no choice, Belle. That pretty little tune is all we have to offer them.'

So it was that on 9th August 1907 at the Palace Theatre, Plymouth, Gertie Gitana first sang the song that was destined to become synonymous with her name. It was an instant hit and became such an essential part of her repertoire that for the rest of her life she could not make a public appearance without having to sing 'Nellie Dean'.

Even on that first night as the audience left the theatre they could be heard humming the refrain of 'Nellie Dean'; although they had not yet learned the words the music stayed with them. That pretty little song became so popular with audiences everywhere that before long it was sung in every English-speaking country in the world. It was sung in the trenches during the Great War when

Gertie Gitana was dubbed the 'Tommies' Favourite Song Bird'.

It was hardly surprising that 'Nellie Dean' should find a special place in the hearts and minds of the masses, especially the boys in the trenches. As in all Gertie's songs, the sentiments were simple and sincere and, in the tradition of all good love songs, it clearly says what the individual finds difficult to express in his own words.

It surely is a simple tune and anyone might be excused for thinking that it must be an easy one to master. That is probably why it was so readily taken up and sung in every public house in the land, but the treatment given it by the drunks at turning-out time was far removed from the sensitive rendition offered by Gertie.

Through the years its popularity never waned and whenever she heard the delicate refrain being murdered on a Saturday night as they wailed out the final notes, sounding more and more like an old gramophone in need of cranking-up, Gertie would say, 'Just listen to what they're doing to poor old Nellie.' Yet she did not really mind. The unpretentious little song was one of her greatest hits and the common people took it to their hearts just as they had taken its singer to their hearts. Gertie was of the people, for the people, and she never forgot her own humble origins.

In the years that followed, the 'Idol of the People' continued to tour and play to full houses in every theatre throughout the land. It was time to record some of her most popular numbers such as 'Nellie Dean' and 'Silver Bell'.

The process of recording was in its infancy and it was no easy task for the performer, who had to sit facing an acoustical horn in those long ago days before microphones. The shellac discs had a recording time of just two and a half minutes, maximum, which meant that the entire performance had to be completed within that time. If, in some instances, the performer appeared to increase the tempo towards the end of a recording it was because they were doing just that in order to fit it within the allotted time.

Of course the sound reproduction of those early recordings left a lot to be desired and it is almost impossible to judge fairly any voice merely by listening to the old seventy-eight recordings. Even when newly pressed they could not give a faithful reproduction of the singer's voice, and if the voice seemed to waver somewhat it was more likely to be due to the shortcomings of the mechanism of the recording equipment rather than the poor technique of the performer. Nevertheless, it is surprising how good many of those recordings still sound today, despite the wear and tear they have suffered through the years.

When 1914 saw the advent of war, patriotic songs, designed to encourage recruitment, flooded the market: songs such as 'We don't want to lose you, but we think you ought to go'. Many female artistes dedicated their energies and charms to promoting these songs and the sentiments they were designed to engender. Many male performers who were exempt from active service because of disability would also put a great deal of effort into the recruiting programme. Gertie always refused to have anything whatsoever to do with recruitment. She was no pacifist but she fervently believed that such matters were for politicians and statesmen, not entertainers. Whilst she supported the war effort and freely gave of her time to raise money for it, her conscience would not allow her actively to persuade young men to go to war and almost certain death.

One of the photographs sold to raise money for war effort

GERTIE GITANA

One of the photographs sold to raise money for war effort

GERTIE GITANA

One of the photographs sold to raise money for war effort

As well as giving charity concerts, Gertie spent endless hours signing photographs of herself which were sold to raise money for Sir Oswald Stoll's 'War Seal Mansions'. This was a scheme designed to raise money for the provision of housing for disabled ex-servicemen and their families. She would utilise any spare moment at home or between theatre performances to do this. The demand for her photographs became so overwhelming that it soon became physically impossible for them all to be signed by hand and later editions had to bear a rubber-stamped signature.

She gave generously of herself, never refusing any request to entertain wounded servicemen in hospitals and never requesting any payment. She was responsible for the dispatch of many thousands of parcels of tobacco, cigarettes, chocolate, in fact any comfort that might make life a little less dire for the troops at the front.

The original Forces' sweetheart, Gertie received sacks of mail from the men in the trenches during those bitter war years. They carried her photograph next to their hearts and those who did not have a girl of their own at home wrote to Gertie. Many were addressed simply to 'Gertie Gitana, Somewhere in England'. They all reached their destination and each and every letter was read and replied to. Gertie was only too aware of the fact that many of the young men who had penned those letters were probably dead by the time she read them. Many of her photographs were returned, blackened by gunshot and countersigned by a pal of the dead soldier in the trenches.

There was one particularly poignant letter which Gertie received:

Dear Madam,

I am enclosing herewith a gift in the shape of a brooch. During the war my brother was serving in the Machine Gun Corps and on one of his leaves left a sealed request with my mother to be opened should anything happen to him. Unfortunately, during the April offensive he was wounded and reported missing.

We have never heard what has happened. The War Office have presumed his death from 14th April 1918. I will quote from his letter which will, I am sure, make quite plain the motive of this unusual gift.

'It is also my last wish that, should the above (his death) come to pass that I desire a present in the shape of a gold ring or brooch to be sent to Miss Gertie Gitana at whichever London music hall where she might be playing as a token of respect and profound admiration for the cleverest lady artiste in vaudeville.'

My brother, Alfred George Leonnard Roberts, invariably went to the hall in London at which you were appearing and had a high regard both for you and your performance. I hope the above is sufficient explanation for what appears to be a rather unusual procedure in approaching one who is unknown personally to the donor.

Although Gertie enjoyed other musical successes such as 'When I Leave the World Behind', which was written for her by Irving Berlin, none would ever match the popularity of 'Nellie Dean'.

It was during the war, in 1917, that Gertie was asked to play principal boy in the pantomime *Puss in Boots* at the Olympia Theatre in Liverpool. Although she was not new to pantomime, having already played the title lead in *Red Riding Hood* with Florrie Ford as principal boy, the idea of Gertie as a principal boy was somewhat of an anomaly. She was small and essentially feminine and, until then, the part of principal boy had always been played by the tall and gutsy, slap-my-thigh school of lady performer. Needless to say, Gertie rose to the occasion and made the part her own.

In her suede tunic and thigh length boots she certainly looked the part. Listening to her witty interpretation of 'My Dusky Princess' it is easy to picture her on stage. Her dainty little mannerisms so characteristic of her femininity were now being used to illustrate the persona of a boy. So skilfully done – a slight change of stance, a certain tilt of the head, introducing a little cheekiness, adding just a little more cockiness, and she succeeds totally in convincing everyone that she is the archetypal principal boy. The gamine character that she so successfully created utterly delighted her audiences and fellow actors alike. They showed their appreciation on the last night when the company, led by the chorus, carried her shoulder high round the stage to tumultuous applause.

Puss in Boots

Young Gertie
(By kind permission of The Theatre Royal, Hanley)

The end of the war saw the efflorescence of the motion picture industry and the music halls began to feel the pinch as audiences, eager to experience this new phenomenon, steadily drifted away. Gertie was still packing them in, she was everyone's 'Darling'. She never forgot the fact that it was her fans who had made her success possible and she never let them down. She had time for everyone and even after a late evening show it was nothing for her to stand for an hour or more in the rain signing autographs for her adoring fans.

Gertie continued to tour successfully accompanied by Auntie and Uncle O'Connor until November 1923 when tragedy struck.

Gertie was topping the bill at the Leeds Empire when Uncle Jimmy became suddenly and seriously ill. Belle and Gertie sat with him throughout that first night of his illness. In silence, with only the flickering embers of the coal fire to light the room, their only movements were to wipe the moisture from his brow. He was no better next day and for the first time in her long association with the O'Connors Gertie went to the theatre alone, leaving Belle to care for her husband.

The following day saw no improvement; in fact, Jimmy was much worse, he had contracted pneumonia. Gertie called her agent to arrange for a deputy so that she could stay with Belle and support her through the crisis.

That night Jimmy's condition continued to deteriorate and the two women watched helplessly as he drifted from delirium into coma. He died the following day. He was fifty-seven years old.

A pall of depression settled on them after Jimmy's death. Gertie cancelled all her engagements for an indefinite period, unable to face the thought of returning to the theatres which held so many memories of happier times. She was as devastated as Belle by Jim's untimely death and touring without him was unthinkable.

This situation might have continued indefinitely but for George Barclay, Gertie's agent at the time. After the funeral he telephoned to say that he had booked her to appear at the Finsbury Park Empire and she was to commence the following Monday. Still grieving and unable to think clearly, Gertie refused to discuss work and quickly replaced the receiver before Barclay had a chance to argue.

Once she had had time to reflect, and there was little else for her to do, Gertie realised that the mourning could not last forever. Jimmy was dead, life must go on. George Barclay had made it easier by making the decision for her.

When Belle heard of Gertie's intention to resume work she was appalled but common sense prevailed as Gertie remained adamant. Come what may, they must return to some sort of normal life. Moping at home was unproductive and finally, if Belle refused to accompany her, she would go to the theatre alone. Then she telephoned Barclay to tell him that she would indeed be ready to make her next appearance at the 'Park' the following week.

There can be no doubt that Gertie found that first night difficult. It was surely the hardest thing she had ever had to do but sheer determination got her through it, somehow, and in so doing she convinced herself, and Belle, that life could go on without Jimmy.

It was customary for music hall people to cling together in times of adversity and there was no shortage of caring friends to rally round and offer support and comfort throughout this sad time. Many fellow artistes called to offer sympathy and help. However, there was one well-meant piece of advice which did not please Belle.

After Gertie had finished her act that first night at the 'Park' there was a knock on her dressing room door and Rosie Lloyd (Marie Lloyd's sister) entered. She addressed Gertie, 'I didn't speak to you at rehearsal, dear, because I know how you must feel, but now you have done your first show I had to pop in to say that all the family send their love. Bear up both of you, it happens to us all (Marie had died the previous year). Jimmy looked after both of you for years, now it's up to you. You ought to find yourself a husband, Gertie. There are plenty of nice fellows around. You could take your pick, any day.'

When Rosie left, Belle turned to Gertie, clearly upset. 'Some people think that having a husband solves every problem.' But, although Rosie's comments had angered Belle, they certainly made Gertie stop and think. It was not such a bad idea. She had been protected, over protected, by the O'Connors for most of her childhood and all her adult life. She was now thirty-six years old and so far had devoted her entire life to pleasing others. 'Maybe I will marry,' she murmured, half to herself. 'After all, there's no reason why I shouldn't.' That did nothing to smooth Belle's ruffled feathers as she spat back, 'Have you anyone particular in mind?'

Noticing the edge to Auntie's voice, Gertie tried to placate her. 'Of course not. But if I did meet someone nice, well, you never know. One thing you can be sure of, Auntie dear, there will always be a place for you.'

Belle refused to be comforted. 'No thank you. I've heard too many jokes about mothers-in-law. It never works. I would buy myself a nice little house. I'd be all right.'

Typically, Gertie put her own feelings to one side and gave Belle a hug. 'Well, we'll see.'

Gertie was working the London halls on a 'Vellum Contract'. This was a special contract which spread over seven years. In each single year twenty-six weeks were appropriated to specified theatres. The contract happened to be printed on vellum paper, hence its name. Because of the competition between the theatre managements to secure the top-line stars of the day for their halls, the London Theatres of Varieties had created the contracts so that the popular stars who attracted the large audiences would be bound to play their halls. There was a bar clause which prevented those on the vellum contract from appearing at any rival theatre.

Although the managements believed the contracts to be favourable to themselves, they discovered a major flaw when some artistes abused the security which the contract provided, becoming lazy and churning out the same old material time and again. There was no clause which afforded the management any redress, unless the artistes concerned broke their contracts. There were many ploys which could be and were used to facilitate such a situation.

A star who had been used to top billing would suddenly find himself in small type at the bottom of the bill and given the poorest spot in the running order of the programme. Others might be allocated dressing rooms at the top of the building, usually reserved for artistes of lower status. One cruel trick was to give a performer double engagements, making it impossible for the one concerned to fulfil both commitments and so be accused of breach of contract.

The ever-increasing threat from the growing popularity of the film industry meant that everyone had to be on their toes and it forced theatre managers to diversify in order to win back audiences who were becoming disenchanted with the old music hall routines. Cissie Williams was the head booker for Moss Empires, and she approached Gertie apropos working in a revue rather than continuing with her long-term contract with Moss Empires as a single act. Although Gertie was still playing to full houses, Cissie thought that her talents would be put to better use if she played the lead in a musical comedy which Norman Lee had written, entitled 'Nellie Dean'. Gertie had refused similar invitations in the past but she allowed herself to be persuaded and finally agreed to accept Cissie's suggestion.

The show opened at the Kilburn Empire, a theatre which became Gertie's own property some years later, and enjoyed a good two-year run.

Flushed with this success Norman Lee wanted to follow it up with another revue; again he took the title from one of Gertie's popular songs and he wrote 'Dear Louise'.

Gertie, probably a pantomime costume

Gertie, probably a pantomime costume

CHAPTER 3

MY BOY BILL

The young man shuffled nervously from one foot to the other as he began to wonder what had induced him to attend this audition. After all, he already had a job in a revue, 'Round the Clock', which was due to open the following Monday. If it had not been for the insistence of his agent he would never have considered putting himself through what was always for him a nerve-racking ordeal. Besides, he could see a queue of at least forty young hopefuls ahead of him and it seemed that each and every one of them was better looking than himself and probably more experienced into the bargain.

Having decided that there was no point in wasting any more time, he was about to leave when an old acquaintance detained him and they started chatting. Suddenly Don Ross heard his name called and he 'was on'.

Norman Lee liked the style of this young man and asked him to wait until the others had left. Don was then told about the part he had just auditioned for, the male lead in a new revue, 'Dear Louise'. This was a great opportunity for any young man. He would be supporting a big star and appearing in the number one theatres. An appointment was made for Don to meet the leading lady of the show. When Don explained that he was already booked to open in a show the following Monday, Norman Lee brushed aside such trivialities. 'We can get you out of any previous commitments if you are accepted for this role. However, it isn't entirely up to me. You must bear this in mind, Miss Gitana has the final word.'

That first meeting between Gertie Gitana and Don Ross is described in his own words:

Don as a young man

The following night a telegram arrived asking me to go to Sheffield to meet Miss Gitana at the Hippodrome on Thursday at 11.00 a.m. The morning was wet and wretched, I felt nervous and thoroughly out of sorts. When I arrived it was too early for the appointment so I walked from the station to the theatre. Through the open door of a public house by the stage door I could see a fire burning in the grate. It looked very cosy and although I didn't want a drink I went in and ordered a Guinness and sat by the fire, drinking it slowly . . .

The stage door keeper knew of my appointment and told me to wait on stage for Miss Gitana. I went along the passage, through the big iron door marked 'STAGE, NO SMOKING', and found myself in the cavern of gloom I knew so well. One pilot light cast its shadows on the stage and as I walked towards the footlights I could see the rows and rows of seats in the darkened auditorium. Few places look less romantic than an empty theatre.

The red-haired lady I had seen in London (Belle O'Connor) came down the centre aisle accompanied by a petite woman. She had glistening dark hair, the bluest of blue eyes and a smile that revealed perfect white teeth.

'So you are Mr Ross. I am Gertie Gitana. My aunt, Mrs O'Connor, tells me you sing and dance very well and I expect you can act quite a bit, can't you? Please don't be nervous, just take your time and relax.'

She called to the stage manager, 'Fred, this young man is auditioning for me, please keep everyone out until we have finished.'

Her kindness and understanding put me completely at my ease. I gave full sympathy to the ballad I sang and my legs swung easily into the dance.

After Don had completed his routine the two women went up onto the stage. Gertie was sure that Don was the right choice for the part but Auntie was not quite so sure at that point. 'You smell of drink. Do you always drink so early in the morning?' As soon as Don explained about his ordeal of nerves before the audition they laughed and the business details were later finalised over a cup of coffee with Auntie's full approval.

That was no mean feat. Everyone in the business knew that in order to get to Gertie one had first to get past Auntie and Don had succeeded in doing that from the word go. He was a charming young man and Auntie was as susceptible to a little charm as the next woman.

From the moment the rehearsals for 'Dear Louise' began Don and Gertie were thrown together for every working minute of every day. Norman Lee concentrated on rehearsing the rest of the cast whilst Don and Gertie performed their rehearsals in another room. Always under the eagle eye of Auntie Belle, of course.

The story of 'Dear Louise' is a simple one of youthful romance. Two young men, one rich, one poor, are both in love with the same girl. In the true romantic tradition and to the delight of the audience the poor boy wins the hand of Louise.

The poor boy, played by Don, is called Billy Rodgers in the show. In the days when people, even theatre people, were more formal than today it was not considered quite correct to call mere acquaintances, even if they were colleagues, by their christian name and Don would never have dreamed of addressing someone of Gertie's standing in so familiar a manner. Although Gertie was senior to Don in every respect, she could not bring herself to call him Don. At the same time it would have been too formal for her to refer to him continually as Mr Ross, especially when they were working so closely together. Don played the part of Billy and so it seemed quite natural to Gertie that she should continue to call him Billy off stage as well as on. That was how Don Ross became Billy Rodgers and Gertie never referred to him by any other name. For the rest of her life she called Don, Bill or Billy. Everyone else adopted this form of address too and even after 'Dear Louise' Don was known as Bill or Billy to all his friends and associates. Don himself adopted the name Billy Rodgers professionally for a time after 'Dear Louise' had finished its run. The name seemed lucky and in many ways it was a lucky day for Don when he accepted that role of Billy Rodgers.

It was on 20th September 1926, Don's twenty-fourth birthday, that 'Dear Louise' opened at the Grand Theatre, Clapham. It proved to be every bit as successful as Gertie's previous revue, 'Nellie Dean', and included such popular songs as 'Let me Call You Sweetheart', 'When Your Hair has Turned to Silver', and 'I'll be Loving You Always'. It played in all the London music halls until Christmas and the following year saw them touring the provinces before returning to London. Although Don Ross was as yet unknown and Gertie was a star, they shared equal billing for the show. Gertie was eager for Don to do well and

Gertie (dedicated to Bill/Don)

Don and Gertie in 'Dear Louise'

arranged for him to have the most romantic, the best songs in the show.

Belle, an enthusiastic card player, would invite Don to wherever she and Gertie happened to be staying to join them for supper and a game of cards after the show. Gertie and Don would take Belle's little dogs for their evening walk before he returned to his lodgings. The two were getting to know each other very well.

One of the scenes in the show required that Don and Gertie make their appearance on a balcony high above the stage. The preparation for that scene necessitated that they climb steep ladders and wait together on a small platform for their cue to enter into audience view on the balcony. They were always on the platform long before they need be. This became their private area, the only private meetings they could count on, away from the rest of the world, to talk, secure in the knowledge that they could not be overheard or interrupted. They were already in love, indeed it had been love at first sight for both of them, now they were getting to know each other and delighting in every stolen minute.

Although Gertie was almost fifteen years older than Don, the age difference never mattered to either of them. Probably because she was so slim and dainty Gertie had never looked her age and she certainly did not feel that she was older than Don, who was mature for his age. Having left home at seventeen to join a group of gentlemen acrobats run by Papa Cragg, he had grown up quickly. Through sheer hard work Don had learned and perfected the most intricate acrobatic feats under Papa Cragg's instruction. Unlike Gertie, Don had known hard times; always having to fend for himself, he had had to make his own way in the world. There had never been any caring Aunt or Uncle O'Connor to manage his career.

It had been a lifelong ambition for Don and a personal victory when he finally plucked up the courage to inform his parents that he was about to leave home to join Papa Cragg's Gentlemen Acrobats. When his mother enquired how acrobats could possibly be regarded as gentlemen, Don replied, 'Because instead of wearing pink tights and leotards they work the act in full evening dress!'

Although his parents had expected greater things of their youngest son, they wished him well as he set out with sixty-eight pounds in his pocket. This was his young life's savings culled from a short stint in journalism and a year's apprenticeship in stockbroking. Don's father had pushed him into work when he consistently failed to make progress at school, not because he was in any way stupid but because Don's heart and mind were and always had been on the stage. He thought nothing of walking the four miles from his home to Leicester's Central Library to read the current copy of *The Stage* from cover to cover before walking the four miles home again. One of his first idols had been Gertie Gitana and his father had taken him to the music hall to see her or Marie Novello, considering them to be the only performers suitable enough for a young boy to spectate.

The romance between Don and Gertie flourished off stage as well as on and he recalls the first time he was invited to visit Gertie in her own home at Woodberry Down in North London.

I was very excited, for apart from my regard for its owner, the house had a place in theatrical history. It had been built for Mrs Sarah Lane, a great figure of the Victorian music hall, who owned the Britannia Theatre, Hoxton. Her ambition had been to make it the Drury Lane of the East End and she certainly succeeded. She was also a lady bountiful and greatly loved by the poor people of the area in which the Britannia stood.

'Kingscliffe' was a double-fronted Victorian style house. A short path from the massive front gates led to an imposing portico and heavy oak door. The house stood in considerable grounds. A large balcony at the back overlooked formal flower beds and a tennis court. On the other side of the lawns stood a wall which ran along the Seven Sisters Road.

Stepping through the front door, one came into a large square hall furnished in oak. The dresser had a fine array of blue and white china on display. There were also oak settles and on the long brickwork mantlepiece were several fine quality Toby jugs. To the right was the dining room and opposite was a small morning room and magnificent drawing room. It was just the sort of room people would picture as being owned by a music hall star. Forty feet long, twenty feet wide, ending in a huge half circular window that overlooked the lawns.

The walls were painted a soft cream but interspersed with panels of old rose brocade, each panel framed in an ornamental carved wood frame tipped with gilt. The Chinese carpet was in matching colour, a delicate shade of old rose. The antique French furniture was of exquisite quality and design. Gertie's collection of rare miniature snuff boxes was displayed on an ornate table. A large cabinet was filled with a collection of beautiful ivories as well as handsome pieces of Dresden and Meissen china. Two huge fireplaces and large crystal chandeliers gave the room a grand look. Gertie was reclining on a fine Louis chaise longue, reading a magazine and eating chocolates. She would take a bite from a chocolate and if she didn't like it she would drop it into a glass bowl by her side. Her preference was for hard centres and I remember thinking what an awful waste of expensive chocolates!

Gertie loved chocolates. It was the one indulgence she allowed herself, she never drank alcohol or smoked, but her chocolate-eating was confined to Sunday, the one day in the week she could call her own. Because chocolate has a tendency to thicken in the throat and adversely affect the voice, she never touched it when she had to sing.

It was inevitable that the question of marriage should arise sooner or later and Gertie was delighted when Don presented her with an engagement ring, a sapphire with two diamonds set in platinum. Don noticed the large diamond on Gertie's other finger which made his ring look rather less significant but, at the same time, he knew that Gertie would treasure his ring more. She was not one to be impressed by great riches for their own sake. Money held little importance for Gertie because she had always had enough for her needs and more. She took it for granted. Unlike Don, Gertie had never known what it was to be hard up.

Don was perplexed and a little hurt when Gertie insisted that their engagement should remain their secret, for the time being at least. He had wanted to shout it from the rooftops, she decided that it was better to wait for an 'opportune moment' before making the news public. Even Auntie was kept in the dark and as they continued their tour with 'Dear Louise' Gertie wore Don's ring on a ribbon round her neck and out of sight.

Although Don complied with Gertie's wishes, he was nevertheless upset.

Whilst it was perfectly reasonable to maintain their privacy during their tour with 'Dear Louise', Don did not welcome the thought of press intrusion any more than his fiancée, he could not understand why Gertie was so reluctant to tell Auntie. There was no-one closer to Gertie and there could only be one reason for this sudden shyness, she was either afraid or ashamed to break the news to Belle. Don had established a close relationship with Belle by this time and all kinds of notions flitted through his mind but he respected Gertie's wishes and remained silent.

'Dear Louise' finished its run in Edinburgh in December 1927 and, although the management wanted to stage another revue, Gertie decided that it was time for her to return to variety. Don was booked to perform in a revival of 'Mumming Birds', the Fred Karno sketch that had launched Charlie Chaplin. Don was billed as Billy Rogers and enjoyed considerable success with that engagement.

In control, as always, Belle suggested that Don should find himself a female partner and Gertie agreed. It would be easier for him to get work as a double act. After advertising in *The Stage* they found a suitable partner, a beautiful blonde. She was a fully trained, all-round dancer specialising in acrobatic work and should be a perfect partner for Don. Although she looked older, Joy Dean was barely sixteen but intensive training had developed her physique. She and Don rehearsed their routine for hours every day. Belle was a hard taskmaster and always supervised these sessions and Don welcomed her advice. At the end of a hard day she would say, 'That's enough. Get yourselves cleaned up and I'll take you out for a nice meal.'

It was during one of those 'nice meals', at the 'Trocadero' in Piccadilly, that Don decided to grasp the nettle and tell Belle about their engagement. Joy had already left the party, just the three of them remained at the table and Don plunged in feet first.

'Auntie, what would you say of a man who had given his girl an engagement ring and she refuses to wear it?'

'If I were the fellow, I'd say she didn't love me.'

'But this girl does love me.'

Belle must have realised what was happening even before Gertie interjected, 'It's me, Auntie. I'm the girl.'

Don and Joy

Belle should not have been too surprised. She had spent every working hour with them both for many months as well as sharing their social lives. She was an astute woman and it is inconceivable that she could have been oblivious to the romance which had blossomed quite literally under her very nose.

Belle shrugged her shoulders, 'It's your own business,' quite rightly even if it was said somewhat grudgingly.

If Gertie had felt any relief now that at last the news had been broken it was to be short lived; she was unaware of the storm that was about to follow. Don ordered her to wear her ring and declared that the wedding would take place on the twenty-fifth of June.

Belle, realising that there was no going back now, reproached Gertie, 'I think you might have told me!'

Gertie was even more surprised than Belle, she and Don had never discussed dates, but she concealed her own feelings and supported Don, 'Billy wanted to tell you, Auntie, but knowing that you'd be upset I kept putting it off.'

'Why should I be upset? It's none of my business. It's your affair.' Nevertheless, Belle could not resist venting a little spite, 'As long as you don't mind people laughing at you. A woman of forty marrying a mere boy!'

Don was quick to retaliate and many angry words were exchanged. Belle accused Don of wanting Gertie for her money and he was not slow to point out that Belle herself might be found guilty of the same fault. Not only that but if the O'Connors had not been so over protective and selfish Gertie would have had the opportunity to marry long before now. They were harsh words but Don knew that Belle could take it.

When that argument petered out Belle tried a different tack, determined to have the last word: 'What about the religious angle? Gertie was brought up as a Roman Catholic and her mother won't be pleased if her daughter marries outside the Church. You are Church of England.'

Gertie must have felt like a rag doll pulled this way then that, being torn apart by two spoilt children. It was all the more painful because the people involved in the wrangle were the two that she loved most. Incapable of knowingly hurting anyone herself, she remained resolute. Although she had been protected from many of life's harsh realities, probably never having to make a decision entirely on her own, certainly never without advice from Belle or Jimmy O'Connor, she was not lacking in determination and she was determined to have her way in this matter. If Belle had thought that she might dissuade Gertie by introducing the 'religious angle' or even make her think again, she was wrong.

Gertie had remained on the sidelines until now. Belle's final comments were too much and, breaking her silence, Gertie turned her sad blue eyes on Belle. 'You really have thought of everything. That never occurred to us. If I don't care one way or the other, I don't see why my mother should.' Gertie, quite rightly, had the final word.

Delighted now that the matter was out in the open, Don set about making the wedding arrangements but there were many hurdles still to be overcome. Don was prepared to marry Gertie in the Catholic Church but when he approached the priest at the Church of the Holy Rosary he was told that he must first take religious instruction and that would take at least three months. When Don explained that because of their business commitments he and Gertie must be married on the twenty-fifth of June, it was the only date available to them both, the priest turned away. 'I cannot help you.'

Gertie had never been fanatical about her religion, it had always been a private, personal thing. She might even make a joke about it or criticise certain aspects of Catholicism but she would never tolerate any derisory comments about the church from non-Catholics. Her religion was important to herself and she had never asked or expected Don to change his religion for her. When he told her what the priest had said she agreed that their only alternative was to marry in the Church of England.

Wishing to keep the wedding as quiet and as dignified an affair as possible, there were no press or public announcements. Don put up the banns in St Olave's, a quiet little church just a few hundred yards from Gertie's house, 'Kingscliffe'. Neither of them believed that anyone would connect the name Gertrude Mary Astbury with Gertie Gitana. Both families were informed as well as a few close friends and all were given strict instructions to 'keep quiet' about the forthcoming event.

After finishing her current tour of Bristol and Birmingham Gertie returned to her London home on the evening of Friday, 22nd June. That gave her two days to rest and prepare for her wedding, which was to take place on the following Monday. She and Don were relaxing at 'Kingscliffe' on the Saturday afternoon when the telephone rang. Gertie answered it and Don heard her say abruptly, 'No, there is no wedding,' before quickly replacing the receiver.

'That was the editor of the *Sunday Graphic* asking if Billy and I were to be married on Monday. I was so taken aback I just said no. He then said that tomorrow's issue of *The People* will have as its front page headline, 'GERTIE GITANA MARRIES TOMORROW' and it was unfair that one paper should be given information that was denied to others.'

That was just the beginning. The telephone rang a few minutes later, then again and again. Capable Belle took over: 'Mr Ross and Miss Gitana are out. I am the housekeeper and I don't know anything about it.' That became her standard reply to the barrage of calls from journalists demanding information. It was inevitable that before long the house would be surrounded by newspaper reporters.

Gertie had planned a restful weekend after a busy work schedule, she was tired and naturally keyed up about the wedding. Now it seemed that all their hopes for a private ceremony were to be dashed. It was totally out of character for Gertie but she was unable to hold back the tears any longer. It was the first time that Don had seen her weep off-stage and it upset him to see his dear Gertie so distraught but he had an idea, a way of beating the publicity.

That same afternoon Don took Gertie to see the priest at St Olave's and explained their problem. Would it be possible for him to marry them tomorrow instead of Monday as previously planned?

Although he was sympathetic, the priest was doubtful. Sunday was his busiest day. 'I don't like to refuse you, Miss Gitana. You have always been more than generous and helpful to this church which is not even yours, but . . .'

Gertie apologised for the inconvenience and turned her brilliant blue eyes to meet his. 'I know you are busy and what we ask is difficult, but I don't want our wedding day turned into a circus, because that is what it will be if it takes place on Monday as all the newspapers are predicting.'

No doubt the priest did not relish the idea of his church being inundated by dozens of reporters and he agreed to marry the couple quietly the following day at two o'clock in the afternoon.

Don describes his own final preparations for that special day:

On the Sunday morning I took especial care with my toilet and dressed carefully in my new dark brown suit (the one Gertie liked best). I scraped the soles of my new brown shoes with a nail file and ran for the bus that would take me to Gertie's house and our wedding. It was hardly a romantic type of vehicle to transport me to the scene of one of the great events of my life, but I did wonder what the other passengers would think if they knew I was going to my wedding and that I was marrying the 'Idol of the People' – Gertie Gitana! You never know who rides on a bus, do you?

Don was such an eager bridegroom that he never gave any thought to the superstitious notion that it was unlucky for the bride and groom to meet before the ceremony.

He arrived at 'Kingscliffe' early to find Gertie still in her dressing gown. She opened a bottle of champagne and they drank a toast to their own future happiness. How they must have treasured that quiet time together before walking the few yards to the church to make their vows. Don went in first and Belle walked alongside Gertie. Despite what had gone before there was never any acrimony between them.

The ceremony was just what they had wanted, private and dignified, although they had to disappoint family and friends in order to achieve it.

After a quiet lunch together they took a taxi to the station to meet Gertie's mother. It must have been one of the few, if not the only, occasion when the guests arrived after the wedding ceremony.

When Gertie told her mother, 'It's all over,' Vinnie assumed that the wedding was off until Gertie explained what had happened and why they had been forced to change their original plans. Vinnie was only a little put out when she learned that Gertie had married in the Church of England.

Don and Gertie had succeeded in outwitting the press, even though it had meant disappointing their respective families, but the storm was not yet over. The following day brought an even greater influx of reporters. Newsreel cameras were

Don and Gertie (probably wedding portrait)

set up outside the house and if the telephone had been busy before it became red hot now. Don had to sneak out of the side entrance of the house in order to escape detection when he went to the station to meet his family, who were still unaware that the marriage had already taken place.

There were as many reporters on the train as family members and it was only by the smart manoeuvring of the taxi drivers following instructions from Don that they were able to return to 'Kingscliffe' unmolested. Again they had to use the side entrance.

As soon as everyone was assembled with a glass in their hands Don broke the news, 'We were married yesterday.'

They felt cheated. All those new outfits bought especially for the occasion would have to languish awhile. Vinnie, practical as always, said, 'I would like to know who gave the news to the press.' Don's mother confessed that she had inadvertently let the cat out of the bag. Someone whom she had not realised was a reporter had engaged her in conversation. Vinnie was angry and called her a 'Chattering Magpie'.

Altercations and recriminations were put aside when everyone was invited to partake of the splendid banquet that Belle had prepared for them. The food was perfect and the bridal chairs were festooned with wreaths of smilax and carnations. Belle had even managed to keep the press at bay long enough for the bride and groom to enjoy their day.

When one of the guests mentioned that the press had reported that Don and Gertie would be spending their honeymoon at the Grand Hotel in Brighton, Don quickly responded and stated in a loud voice, 'We were going to stay there until the news got out so I telephoned and cancelled. We will now be staying at the Queen's Hotel in Eastbourne, registered as Mr and Mrs Melvin.'

Don and Gertie had to make an unceremonious exit across the lawn to avoid the gathering of journalists who were still camped at the front of the house. They succeeded in getting away unnoticed.

When they eventually arrived at their hotel Don ordered tea to be served on their balcony overlooking the sea. At last, the couple could breathe easily but as Gertie began to pour the tea the sound of voices singing 'Nellie Dean' drifted on the afternoon air. Gertie almost dropped the teapot, 'Oh no! This is too bad.

We've been here twenty minutes and they've found us already.' Don was able to reassure her after looking over the balcony. It was only a group of day trippers passing by and pure coincidence that they happened to be singing that particular song at that time. After all the trials of the previous week Don and Gertie were at last able to enjoy a quiet honeymoon, alone.

The time soon sped by and a return to London and their respective work schedules came all too soon. Although they were working in different theatres, Don and Gertie always made a point of spending their evenings together when, after their last show, they would return to 'Kingscliffe' for a quiet supper. Don remembers, 'We were unspeakably happy.'

They decided to sell 'Kingscliffe' and move to a smaller house when Gertie's housekeeper expressed her desire to retire. The sale was completed within three days, even before they had time to think of looking elsewhere. Rosie Lloyd suggested, 'Have a look at Golders Green. Marie liked it very much. A nice area, not too far from the West End.'

They looked and fell in love with a house named 'Craigmore'. Belle agreed that it was indeed a lovely house and the location was perfect but she had found herself a house in the same area. Not too far away but not too near. 'I don't want to be a mother-in-law.'

Gertie felt more than a little hurt by Belle's attitude and both she and Don tried to make her understand that they really did want her to stay with them. No amount of coaxing would induce Belle to change her mind. She went ahead with her plans and moved her furniture into her new house. At the last moment, after many tears and much pleading, Belle agreed to stay with Gertie and Don, but for a trial period only.

Belle never did move into her new house. The 'trial period' was so successful that she rented out her new house and remained at 'Craigmore'.

CHAPTER 4

MR AND MRS ROSS

B efore long the old routine of work was resumed and there was plenty to keep them all busy. The house was well staffed and Belle was always available to help and advise. As before, Gertie was free to concentrate on her rehearsals and performances. She was proud of her new husband and always insisted that as the man of the house he should deal with all business matters. Whatever queries arose Gertie would invariably reply, 'Ask my husband.' Theatre managers would often ask her to make a public appearance, open a bazaar or attend some similar function. The answer was always the same, 'Ask my husband, he's in charge.'

At first Don must have felt as if he were on show to some extent, as everyone wanted to see the young fellow that Gertie had married and she was happy to show him off. Arm in arm he and Gertie would walk on stage, looking radiantly happy, as indeed they were, and join the other artistes who were waiting to rehearse. But there was one occasion when they were reminded that the stage manager had the last word.

Gertie was working at the London Coliseum on a late spot and Don accompanied her to the side of the stage before leaving for his own act elsewhere. Ignoring Don, the stage manager addressed Gertie, 'Who is this?'

'I was just going to introduce you, Mr Crocker. This is my husband.' The stage manager was unimpressed. 'I'm delighted to meet you but I am sorry I do not allow anyone to come onto my stage.' Gertie was upset, 'But this is my husband, Mr Crocker.'

'I know,' Mr Crocker remained civil but firm, 'but I will not have anyone who is not actually engaged in the performance to be on the side of the stage.'

Gertie apologised, 'I'm sorry, Bill. You will have to wait in the dressing room for me.'

Don understood and agreed with Mr Crocker. Although he might have been a little pompous, he was the stage manager and right to insist on correct stage discipline. When the fine old music hall traditions began to fade it was the lack of attention to stage discipline that was particularly evident as visitors were allowed to wander about behind the scenes at will. It became a free for all.

Another sign of slacking had already crept in. Many artistes, wishing to get away quickly after the final curtain on a Saturday night, would have all their costumes and best clothes packed as soon as their turn had finished, in order that they might leave immediately to catch the earliest possible train back to London or the next town where they were billed to appear.

Don and Gertie

This practice was roundly condemned by the manager of the Brighton Hippodrome. The clientèle who frequented his theatre deserved better and a notice to that effect was posted in every dressing room:

LADY ARTISTES are requested to note
that the audience at the second performance
on a Saturday night is undoubtedly the
smartest in this country and they must NOT
therefore pack their best dresses until AFTER
they have made their final stage appearance!

There is no mention as to what instructions, if any, were given the male artistes but Don had always been taught to dress immaculately. A true pro should be as particular about his appearance in the street as on the stage. Don was reminded of this in later years when Randolph Sutton related a tale of how he had been booked to appear at two different venues in the same evening. There was so little time to spare between the two performances that he had to stand up in the taxi which transported him to his last appearance of the evening. When Don asked why he had to stand, Ran replied, 'I didn't want creases in my crotch, you fool!' No performers who took any pride in their appearance would ever sit down whilst wearing their stage clothes.

Don and Joy worked well together and their act was gaining popularity. Belle and Gertie were always there to advise and encourage. Gertie's agent, George Barclay, suggested to her that he could arrange it so that Don and Joy would be booked on all Gertie's programmes, meaning that if a theatre wanted Gertie they would also be obliged to take Don and Joy as a package. Gertie thought hard about it but decided, wisely, that much as she would like Don to tour on the same circuit it would be unfair to all concerned if his act was accepted on any other terms than its own merit.

Developing a new act is not easy. It is never easy to be original, however much talent an artiste may have. It is doubly difficult to establish a new act with a partner, timing is crucial as well as knowing one's partner well, which is only achieved by repetitive rehearsal and many months of working together. Don and

Joy worked extremely hard in perfecting their act and played round the circuits a couple of times. They were becoming known and Auntie Belle decided that it was time to introduce a new element to their already successful presentation. 'Up to now,' she said, 'you have worked on a flat stage. Now, I want you to work on a staircase. It will be difficult at first but its novelty value will make it worth while.' Whatever Don and Joy thought of the idea they never said but dutifully prepared themselves for rehearsing the new routine whilst a large staircase was built to Auntie Belle's specifications. It was a huge construction made of solid wood, fifteen feet wide and fifteen feet high, made in two separate sections which had to be screwed together before each use.

The routine that Belle had devised involved Don performing hock steps, crouching on his hunkers in the manner of a Russian dancer round the flat stage before ascending the staircase, all the time retaining the same position. Once he reached the top he would turn his back on the audience and, placing his hands on the second step from the top, commence his descent performing a series of slow even backs.

Joy's routine included a drum tattoo on points up and down the staircase. Her ballet shoes had steel taps on their points, an innovation in those days which always drew tremendous applause.

Once they had reached the top of the staircase, hopefully at the same time, they would perform a routine of acrobatics to waltz time.

It was an exceptionally difficult routine, one which required months of intensive work to perfect. There would be days when everything went well and they congratulated themselves until the next day when everything seemed to go wrong and successive falls resulted in bruised shins, grazed elbows and a thoroughly despondent mood.

Belle did not allow any setbacks to demoralise her and she would not hear any talk of giving up, 'Never mind. Let's do it again.' And again and again until they were just about perfect.

They were playing at the Wolverhampton Hippodrome when Auntie entered Don's dressing room as he was making-up. It was Saturday night, a few minutes before the commencement of the show. 'The staircase dance is in tonight.'

Don could hardly believe his own ears. 'We can't possibly . . .' he began to protest.

'You can and you will,' Belle insisted. 'You've done it perfectly many times at rehearsal. If it doesn't go in now it never will. I've already given the music to the M.D and told the stage manager.'

That was the final word from Belle and she left the room without waiting for any reply because none was needed. The decision had been made.

Don knew that it was futile to argue with Auntie but he was not at all happy about the situation. Heart thumping, he watched in the wings as the stage hands assembled the staircase. It was as if for the first time he realised the magnitude of the structure and the task he and Joy had before them. It seemed impossible. Joy stood silently beside him. Then their music commenced: this was the point of no return, death or dishonour. They were on.

Don's worst fears were realised when, after perfectly executing his act on the flat stage he hesitated and missed his cue to ascend the staircase. Fortunately, the conductor was a true professional and continued to play another chorus, giving Don the chance to recover his equilibrium and Belle called out from the wings, 'Get up those stairs!'

Belle and Gertie, along with other acts who were waiting their turn to go on, watched with bated breath as Don began to dance up the staircase. It must have seemed like Everest to him, crouched on his hunkers as he began the ascent but he was encouraged by the feeling of support emanating from the wings. All went well until he prepared for the descent. On the second step from the top he missed his footing and tumbled head over heels down onto the stage. Showing amazing presence of mind, he finished with a double somersault facing the audience with both arms outstretched and cried, '*Voilà!*'

He was never quite sure if the audience were convinced that it was all part of the act but he finished to well-deserved applause.

As Joy commenced her dance she must have felt more than a little trepidation but she tip-tapped her way faultlessly to the top of the staircase. However, once on that top step she overbalanced and disappeared from sight. Gertie managed to suppress a cry of alarm whilst those other supporters in the wings looked on in silent horror. A fall of fifteen feet was not to be treated lightly. However, Joy re-appeared on stage, remounted the staircase and bravely completed her part of the act.

At last, the curtain came down and two utterly demoralised dancers limped back to their dressing rooms to do what they could to repair their bruised and battered limbs. Physical injury was not Don's main concern, he felt dispirited and humiliated because he had disappointed Belle. As he and Joy surveyed the personal damage there was a knock on the door and Belle breezed in. 'Not bad for the first time, darlings. Nerves, that's all. It will be all right on Monday at Leeds.' Don and Joy could not believe their ears as they stared at each other, mouths agape. Belle cast a hasty eye over their bruises. 'That's nothing. You've got it on at last. That's all that matters.' And they both knew there was absolutely no point in arguing with Auntie.

It became a constant battle in the early thirties to continue to fill the halls. Since the advent of radio and talking pictures the industry faced growing competition. Theatre managers capitulated by offering their audiences a double top of the bill with two big names for the price of one. Gertie and George Elliott formed a successful partnership and made a big hit at the Empress, Brixton, in January 1930.

Gertie had also been offered a number of weeks work on 'shares' with the management. That meant she had to provide the supporting artistes to appear with her on the bill. This provided Don with an opportunity to exercise his entrepreneurial skills as he took over the management of Gertie's career.

When he was a little boy Don's favourite pastime had been organising and managing his toy theatre, which was set out on the dining room table after Sunday tea. Although his father had encouraged him, his mother had strongly disapproved. It would not have been so bad if Don had wanted to be a serious actor like Tree, but the music hall! She was dismayed by her son's intense interest in jugglers, acrobats, comediennes and singers, all of whom travelled the country sleeping in all kinds of places and mixing with dissolute men and fast women.

Now a childhood dream was about to come true. It was Auntie's idea to invite George Elliott to join them on a long-term basis. George agreed wholeheartedly and it was to be the foundation of a lifelong partnership.

Don had the business side organised immediately. George was to join them on a fifty-fifty basis. He and Gertie would share top billing and, as Don put it to George, 'I'll do all the business side, all you've got to do is let me pay you half the profits at the end of each week.' It was an arrangement which suited everyone.

Together, Gertie and George were an unqualified success. Many theatre managers were interested and requested them to tour their own circuits. There was plenty of work, the takings were good, which meant that Don was able to pay them all good salaries, more than they would have earned working on a flat salary. Don managed the business side of things admirably, leaving Gertie and George free to concentrate on perfecting their act.

Of course, no matter how good a show is there is bound to be the occasional disappointment when the house is not as full as everyone might have expected. One such occasion presented itself when they were appearing at the Olympia in Dublin. After having played to full houses all week, the theatre was almost empty on the Friday night's first house. George was always the one to buoy up flagging spirits with a joke, 'I know what it is, Gertie. A Cardinal is lying in state at one of the churches round the corner and they've all gone to view the body.' Although he did not know it at the time, it happened that George was absolutely right!

Don was invited by George Barclay's Manager, Bob Wade, to see a new comedian who was currently playing at the Camberwell Palace. Bob thought that this young man would be just right to appear with Gertie and George.

It was a strange act. A young man dressed as a gypsy complete with a bandanna tied round his head, he was billed as 'Nedlo, the Gypsy Violinist'. Although his name and dress were inappropriate, the young man showed definite promise.

As soon as he saw him perform Don thought this young man had talent as well as personal charm and, although the gypsy outfit was old hat, he had 'a splendid line of patter'. His real name was Charlie Olden and he had decided that Nedlo (Olden spelt in reverse) was a clever idea as well as being a good stage name. He was advised by George Barclay to get rid of the costume and the name, buy himself a lounge suit and adopt a new title. Ted Ray was one suggestion and as such he never looked back.

Ted Ray became a close friend of Gertie and Don, like one of the family. He married Sybil Stevens, whom he met whilst he was working in one of Don's shows at the Hippodrome, Birmingham, and she was appearing in a revue at the Empire. When their first son, Robin, was born Gertie and Don were godparents to him.

As if fate had decreed it, Don had a turn off. Harry Champion, whom he had already billed to appear at the Southend Hippodrome, was unable to appear, so, on 6th July 1931 Ted Ray made his first appearance. He was paid fifteen pounds for the week's work and was an instant success.

Bob Wade approached Don again, this time to ask if he was interested in forming a partnership. Bob had worked as office manager for George Barclay for fifty years but had become disenchanted after Barclay had reduced his salary for the second time in a year. Bob was just turned sixty and had suffered enough of Barclay's outbursts of temper. He had been running Barclay's office for years and he was sure that he and Don could set up a good business together with Don as agent.

Don was not too sure about the idea. He still enjoyed performing and managing Gertie's business suited him. If Don accepted Bob's offer it would mean his being confined to an office in London and Gertie would be on tour without him. He promised to think about it and let Bob know his decision the following week.

Although Belle and Gertie assured Don that it was a wonderful opportunity for him, he was loth to take the plunge and it was Vinnie who gave the final push. She had just arrived at 'Craigmore' for a few days holiday and, as soon as she heard about the proposition, she was all for it. 'I think it's a good idea. Doing all that hard acrobatic dancing, coming off stage gasping for breath and all that practice, it's enough to kill anybody. He's not getting any younger, he's turned thirty now.'

There was nothing left to say. When Bob telephoned, Don accepted his offer and became an agent.

Bob wanted to open the office at the beginning of July. That gave Don just enough time to find a suitable partner for Joy and snatch a holiday with Gertie before taking up his new position.

Don's office was situated in the heart of theatre land, Gloucester Mansions in Shaftesbury Avenue. Gertie had organised the carpets and furnishings and on the first day she organised an opening day lunch. At one o'clock she and Belle arrived with a steaming hot steak and kidney pudding from their kitchen at 'Craigmore'. The silver, table napkins, crystal, everything that would accompany a dinner at home, were unpacked together with plenty of champagne.

As they were enjoying the meal Jack Marshall, the booker for Stoll's, telephoned, 'Just want to wish you best of luck and also to book something with you on your first day. Who have you got for third turn at Bristol for next week? Robb Wilton? Okay, put him in.'

Gertie hugged her husband, 'Congratulations, darling. You've just booked your first act.'

Don was soon planning a booking tour. The major tours were usually booked from their London offices but there were many privately owned theatres in the provinces which booked acts on the spot. The managements knew and respected Don as an artiste, he had worked often enough in their theatres, now he had to re-introduce himself as an agent. He also knew many artistes who had willingly given their permission for him to offer them to the managers and, even before he started, Don had acquired a sizeable list of good acts on his book. Don always maintained that being Gertie's husband gave him tremendous prestige and opened many doors that otherwise might have been closed to him. That is undoubtedly true but if it were not for Don's own charm and business acumen he could never have achieved the tremendous continuing success which he enjoyed in his own right and which was to earn him the title 'Mr Show Business'.

Whilst on a booking tour of the privately owned theatres in the provinces he was invited by Mr Broadhead, the proprietor of a chain of music halls, to put on a pantomime, *Cinderella*, at the King's Palace, Preston. That was to be followed by a tour of the circuit. Don was so excited about this new challenge that he could not wait to get home to break the good news to Gertie. He went straight from Mr Broadhead's office to the nearest public telephone.

Continuing his booking tour Don travelled to Bolton, Wigan, Birkenhead and Leeds. He was later to become the sole booking agent for the City of Varieties in Leeds and remain so for more than twenty years. After Middlesborough and Hull he returned to London and Gertie, 'Feeling like a conquering hero!'

It was Gertie's idea that they should put on a revue entitled, 'George, Gertie and Ted', George being George Elliott, and Ted Ray who wrote their introductory song, 'George, Gertie and Ted':

> George, Gertie and Ted,
> George, Gertie and Ted.
> Our aim is to bring much pleasure to you,
> For our entertainment is novel and new.
> All trouble has fled,
> And you will be happy instead.
> Don't worry 'bout tomorrow
> 'Cos it never comes they say,
> Our troubles are like bubbles, we can blow them away.
> Just sing this little song and you are bound to feel okay
> With George, Gertie and Ted.

Ted fancied himself as a songwriter and wrote several other lighthearted ditties for the show as well as a big production scene, where they each did an impersonation of other music hall stars such as George Formby Sr. and G. S. Melvin. Ted would wear drag and sing, 'I'm Happy When I'm Hiking'.

Together they gave audiences something new and the revue ran for four and a half years. Don managed all the bookings for 'George, Gertie and Ted', of course, and one of the reasons for the show's huge success was the tremendous input of enthusiasm and energy from all concerned.

Don had discovered a troupe of girls, 'Harry Firth's Dainty Maids'. They were good-looking girls and fine acrobats but Don did not like their title; however, no amount of persuading would induce Mr Firth to change it so 'Dainty Maids' they had to remain.

Gertie was an excellent seamstress and played a major part in the costuming of the show whilst Don organised the scenery and script material. They all worked together sharing ideas in the planning of the finished product.

Everything went beautifully until one evening after supper when Don introduced a new idea. He had thought of a perfect song for George, so much so it might have been written for him, 'Lily of Laguna'. Don had already worked out a stage setting of cotton fields with the girls dressed as mammies. It would be the high point of the show.

For the first time ever George flatly refused a request from Don. 'That was Eugene Stratton's song,' George was angry. 'One thing I have never done, and never will do, is to sing a song that another artiste has made famous.' Don tried to reason with him but George was adamant. He could not do that number.

Belle cut in, 'George, Stratton has been dead for almost twenty years. There's a whole new generation out there who never saw him, they probably don't even remember his name.' It made no difference to George, he could not steal another artiste's song.

Don tried again, 'I understand your feelings, George, and I agree with you, up to a point. I remember you telling me about the time you and Stratton appeared at the Palladium on the same bill. Your individual styles were so different the audience never realised that there were two coon acts on the bill!'

There was a long silence. Then, Gertie began to speak, to no-one in particular. 'Stratton had very little voice as I recall. He sang in a harsh, staccato manner, almost talking the songs. It is strange, when you think of it, Leslie Stewart wrote so many lovely songs for a man who couldn't sing.' Then, turning to George, she said softly, 'You have a lovely voice, George, and you yodel beautifully. Eugene's great strength was his dancing, but you dance well too.' George remained silent, but Gertie was not one to give up easily, 'Go on, George, do the number. It would be great.'

Even the most resolute heart would have found it difficult to resist a plea from Gertie and George finally agreed to sing the song which was to become an essential part of his act. Throughout the remainder of his career George Elliott, the 'Chocolate-Coloured Coon', was associated with the song 'Lily of Laguna', quite as much as Gertie was with 'Nellie Dean'.

Even so he did not agree to the idea without reservations. He insisted that Gertie join him in the dance and finish up as a duet. He was to remain sensitive about the connection with Eugene Stratton and whenever his name was mentioned George was always quick to point out that, whilst Stratton had used the traditional burnt cork make-up of the old minstrel style with the white mouth, his was different. He had never fashioned himself on Stratton.

George's make-up was a work of art. He would hold a tin plate over a candle

Don's favourite portrait of Gertie

flame until it was covered with a film of soot. This was mixed with a brown cocoa-like powder called 'bole'. A little cork was used but he always preferred the champagne variety which Don would often supply. The finishing touches were blue eye-shadow, dark carmine on the lips and powdered rouge on the cheeks. Once the make-up was completed George's face took on a clear milky chocolate-coloured complexion, hence his title, 'Chocolate-Coloured Coon'.

Once 'George, Gertie and Ted' had been successfully launched, Don was able to concentrate on his pantomime. Never having produced such a venture before he wanted this to be different. Don wrote the script himself as well as the accompanying music and a chorus song to 'let down on the sheet' so that the audience could participate. He wanted to dispense with the usual irrelevancies common to pantomime, wishing to remain true to the plot of the original story. He even went so far as to order live rabbits for the woodland scenes and live rats for the fairy godmother to metamorphose into horses to draw the crystal coach.

Don was in his element as he personally supervised all the arrangements, every minute detail from the installation of the scenery and all the props, including the delivery of the crystal coach from the station to the theatre. He watched over the wardrobe mistresses as they unpacked the baskets, making sure that each costume reached the correct dressing room. As he watched all this activity he must have been reminded once again of his childhood days with his toy theatre and himself in sole charge of the performances. The dream had become reality.

At last they were ready to run through the first rehearsal in the theatre with the orchestra. Although the cast were fully versed in their material they had been accompanied by a piano until now, the presence of an orchestra made it more like the real performance. The dress rehearsal followed but Don insisted on another run through before he could be sure that they were really ready for the opening. They had all worked hard at perfecting their individual roles and Don thanked everyone before they finally retired to their dressing rooms. It was past midnight, everyone was very tired.

Mr Broadhead decided to make a noisy entrance; storming down the centre aisle he called out for the entire cast to be brought back on stage, he wanted to see the show. Don tried his utmost to dissuade him, insisting that it was unfair to treat his actors in this way, nevertheless Broadhead got his way and the entire performance was repeated. He found fault with everything and everyone, continually interrupting with loud remarks. Don gritted his teeth, apologised to his cast and thanked them once again at the end of the ordeal. Inwardly seething, Don made to leave the theatre, accompanied by Auntie and Gertie with Mr Broadhead in hot pursuit.

'Now look here, Miss Gitana,' Broadhead was determined to be heard by someone, 'let's not get upset. Have you ever seen a Cinderella like that?' If he thought that Gertie would take his part against her husband he soon found out how wrong he could be, as she turned and fixed him with a cold look. 'Of course I have. What's the matter with her? She's young and pretty as well as being a very good performer. You didn't give her a chance.'

With that the trio turned their backs on Mr Broadhead and drove home in dismal silence, worn out and utterly dejected.

Don was too nervous to watch the first night of his first pantomime. Gertie was there, out front alone whilst Auntie, as always, supervised things back stage. Don paced the length of a passage behind the stage. He was within earshot and as the show got underway what he heard was more than encouraging. The audience laughed long and loudly and the applause came frequently. When it was time to introduce the rabbits, Auntie gave a signal to the stage hands to place them in the tunnels which led onto the stage. The initial reaction from the audience was tremendous and Don listened to the squeals of delight coming from the children. He began to wonder if any of them had ever seen a live rabbit before. It seemed that everything was going even better than he could have imagined until Cinderella made her appearance. Instead of respectful silence the laughter became even more hilarious. A dismayed Don rushed down the side of the stage almost colliding with Auntie. 'You and your damn rabbits,' she howled.

'What are they doing?'

'What do rabbits do? They're misbehaving, all over the stage!'

The little miscreants were eventually rounded up and the show was able to proceed but Don was naturally having second thoughts about allowing the rats to go on. Fortunately, they behaved admirably and won many rounds of applause.

At last, the final curtain and as Don made his way to the stage to congratulate his cast on such a successful first night he was beaten to it by Mr Broadhead. 'A very fine pantomime, ladies and gentlemen. One of the finest I've ever had in any of my theatres.'

Before the next performance Don made a careful inspection of the rabbits and separated the bucks from the does. Only the bucks were allowed on stage next time. His efforts proved to be futile, they still misbehaved. The rabbits had to go.

Although Don's first pantomime proved to be a great achievement and was followed by several more, he decided that pantomime was not his métier after all. The average run would be about six weeks and required much more work than five or six revues which would usually last fifty weeks at least.

CHAPTER 5

AMERICA

In 1935 Don suggested that he and Gertie should visit America. The agency was doing well but he wanted to see some fresh faces, investigate the talent on the other side of the Atlantic. Gertie welcomed the idea and they duly booked their passages on the S.S *Bremen* and sailed for New York.

During the trip they met and soon made friends with an American couple, Ralph Henderson and his wife. Ralph was the Editor of the American *Reader's Digest* and he asked Don what interested him most. When Don said that he wanted to visit Sing Sing prison, a night police court and, most importantly, Minsky's Burlesque Show, Ralph assured Don that he could arrange all those visits for him.

On their first night in New York the Hendersons took Don and Gertie to Lindy's for dinner, where they were introduced to many of the leading artistes of the day. They were made to feel so welcome that it was well after midnight before they arrived at the night police court.

They were stopped at the door by a policeman who insisted that the court was full until Ralph explained that Don and Gertie were from England and the court was the very thing about New York that fascinated them most. There was no longer a problem; anyone from London, England, was welcome.

Don describes the experience which followed:

We moved in to a large brilliantly lit hall with rows of benches on either side of a wide gangway. On a dais at the end of the end of the room, facing us, sat the judge. To his left was the witness box. The lawyers and sundry witnesses sat in front. Although the benches were crowded with onlookers there was a feeling of bareness about the room. The case in progress concerned two street photographers accused of taking and trying to sell pictures of passers by. They pleaded, 'We've done it in Jersey City and had no trouble there.' The judge was unmoved, 'It's against the law in New York City. I fine you twenty dollars. Next case!'

The proceedings followed in a similar vein. An Italian accused of beating his wife in the street pleaded guilty, 'I was wrong. I should have waited till I got home.'

The judge was constrained to hammer continuously with his gavel as the public insisted on chatting to each other, even calling to friends across the room. It was only when Don and Gertie left the court that they realised the cause of a continuous crackling noise that had accompanied the show, a dense carpet of peanut shells!

Their next visit, a guided tour of Sing-Sing, proved to be a chilling experience.

They were greeted by the warden, a frank, hearty little man, who showed them the prison cinema, theatre, chapels for all the religious denominations, and an aviary which housed every kind of bird from a common sparrow to the exotic bird of paradise. In charge of them all was a real 'gor blimey cockney' from London.

Any feeling of cheeriness soon deserted them when they were shown the cells. They were below ground level, small and narrow, each housing four men. These were for long-term prisoners. There were other cells where wealthy prisoners were allowed to buy in their home comforts. However, when they left the prison they were obliged to leave whatever furnishings they had provided for themselves. These prisoners seemed to be as comfortable as anyone could ever be in such surroundings but Gertie and Don felt the sinister undertones, as if violence might break out at any minute.

The warden proudly showed them the death chamber next. Executions were public affairs. The prison received thousands of applications from members of the public to attend an execution and half a dozen were usually admitted. Before the event everyone was given a glass of brandy for the obvious reason.

In a weak moment Don allowed himself to be strapped into the electric chair.

He felt increasingly uncomfortable as the warden proceeded to give a detailed commentary of the last moments of a victim. He pointed to a large switch, the size of a policeman's truncheon, 'That's the one that finishes the job.' Don felt faint and Gertie implored, 'Oh, do be careful, please,' as the warden moved towards the switch.

When Don was finally released the warden took the little party to the refrigerator which was full of coffins.

They had experienced enough of Sing Sing and Gertie was keen to leave but the horrors were not quite over. The way out was through Death Row. The inhabitants, many of whom had been waiting in limbo for years, had no privacy and some screamed abuse at the visitors. Don and Gertie made a hurried exit and thankfully breathed the fresh air again.

Any remaining depression was soon dispelled by their visit to Minsky's. On 42nd Street the Apollo Theatre was filled almost entirely by men. That was hardly surprising because the girls were the main attraction. It was a continuous show of striptease, a chorus of dancing girls and a comedian by the name of Peanuts Bohn.

Don was immediately taken with Peanuts; although he looked quite grotesque, ugly with mobile features and some of the bluest material that he had ever heard, Don recognised that he was a great comedian, but that was not all.

Peanuts had a wife, Kenza Vinton, who performed a stunning strip-tease act. She was tall, graceful and beautiful. Her dignity was unassailable and she had an air of disdain for her audience. Her act was executed with great élan.

By that time Vaudeville was finished in America but many of the large cinemas would put on several acts between the showing of films. Don travelled to Philadelphia, Chicago, Buffalo and Detroit. He visited every theatre in New York, he wanted to see everything. Finally, he found himself at the Opera House in Harlem for 'Amateur Night'.

We usually got there just before the show commenced. The house was packed with an audience revelling in what I thought was a sadistic orgy. How anyone could submit themselves to the kind of humiliation the performers were subjected to I shall never understand. Set up-stage centre was a large tree trunk and as each artiste entered they first touched it before going into their act. Apparently this was an old good luck custom.

The acts were introduced by a master of ceremonies-cum-comedian. If not immediately liked by the audience, a huge hook (something like a shepherd's crook) came from the wings, encircled the poor devil's waist and hauled him off the stage to the frenzied shouts and boos of the audience. If the performer protested and tried to hold his ground the compère would assist physically to speed his exit. On one occasion disapproval was shown by the firing of blank shots from a pistol as a final warning for the artiste to get off the stage.

Although Don thought these proceedings were demeaning for the participants, there was a positive side to the proceedings. There were always agents in the house on the look-out for new talent and any performer who managed to please the audience could be sure of at least one booking. It was a way of getting noticed.

Don's intention was not to book high-salaried entertainers but rather to seek out new and exciting acts for whom he could organise plenty of work in Britain and on the Continent. Peanuts Bohn and his wife, Kenza Vinton, were among those who gave Don sole authority to book them on his side of the Atlantic. Kenza became one of the first strip-tease artistes to appear in the U.K.

When the time came for them to leave, Don and Gertie felt more than a little sad to be saying farewell to so many new-found friends, who had offered them the best hospitality. The trip had been a very successful one for Don. He had met a true cross-section of people. Both he and Gertie were overwhelmed by the number of people who took the trouble to see them off on their homeward journey.

As the S.S. *Bremen* drew away from the quayside Don and Gertie bade a tearful farewell to all their well-wishers. When they finally retreated to their staterooms they found them full of flowers, fruit, wine, chocolates and other gifts from their American friends, who had been strangers but a few weeks before.

As soon as Don returned to London he was planning his next show. Prince Littler, who had recently become head of the Stoll Theatres, was moved by

Gertie's enthusiasm when she told him about Peanuts Bohn. 'You are both good judges of talent, so why not back your hunch? For a start, I'll give you my dates.'

Don and Gertie set about the task of framing a show. It did not take long to contact Peanuts to discuss their proposition. Cables were exchanged and Peanuts arrived to perform in a revue entitled, 'Personality Parade'. Ted Ray had top billing along with Peanuts. The rest of the bill was taken up by American dancers and a pair of Mexican acrobats whose finale was quite amazing. They walked backwards on a tightrope which reached from stage to gallery before descending at full speed maintaining a standing position. A lovely sixteen-year-old singer by the name of Kathleen Moody proved to be a great attraction, she was later to become Mrs Lew Grade.

'Personality Parade' opened at the Empire, Birmingham. It was not the success that Don had anticipated and after twelve weeks he took it off the road. It was a disappointment as individually the artistes were good. Peanuts Bohn was sensational.

Peanuts discussed the failure of the show with Don. He was convinced that if they introduced Kenza Vinton to the British public they would have a show second to none. Peanuts also suggested that there should be no fancy titles. 'Let's be honest, Mr Ross, give them burlesque.' Don agreed and came up with the title 'Don't Blush, Girls'.

The British labour permit regulations allowed foreign artistes a six months' stay only. Until they could arrange for Kenza to make the crossing Peanuts went to live in Paris so as not to waste any of the valuable time allotted to him in the U.K. Gertie and Don continued with the arrangements for the show and visited Paris regularly to keep Peanuts informed of their progress.

When the show was finally ready the only available theatre for a London opening was the Walthamstow Palace. It was notorious as being one of the poorest halls in London for business but 'Don't Blush Girls' changed all that. The Palace saw the biggest takings that it had in years. Other theatre managers clamoured for dates.

Val Parnell, of the Moss Empires and General Theatre Corporation, approached Don. 'I don't particularly care for your show, but Peanuts is a truly great comedian, the show is a sensational success and I must book it for our theatres.'

What does it cost you to run?'

Don was more than a little surprised. 'Why do you ask that?'

'Because I'm going to pay you a salary.'

Don remained wary. 'The production costs and running expenses are my business. I know what this show plays to each week and I'm entitled to get the best salary possible, so what can you offer?'

After some haggling a price was finally agreed upon. Val was to organise the route and contracts and Don was pleased with the profits he received from the agreement.

Peanuts was an instant success with all audiences and Kenza was the first American strip-tease artiste that British audiences had seen. She turned strip-tease into an art. They were so popular with audiences wherever they played that they earned more money than they ever had before, even in the States.

CHAPTER 6

WAR

With Peanuts and Kenza in the show, 'Don't Blush Girls' could not fail. Kenza was beautiful and dignified and she raised strip-tease to an art form. The press loved her.

When the American Embassy announced the date of the last ship to sail from Britain to the United States, together with the information that they could not be responsible for any American citizens who voluntarily remained on British soil after that date, Peanuts and Kenza decided to return to the States.

Don had to find replacements for them and quickly. In London he contacted an excellent young comedian, Roy Lester, and Jean Morris, who was a beautiful young strip-tease artiste. Although Jean was a talented stripper she was not a competent speaker on stage so Phyllis Pleydell, the niece of Rob Wilton, was chosen to fill in the vocal parts.

It turned out to be a very rushed job as Don took the three to South Shields, where Peanuts and Kenza were giving their final few performances before leaving on the last ship for America.

Roy, Jean and Phyllis watched every performance very carefully each evening and followed through by rehearsing during the day. They worked hard and were able to take over smoothly from Peanuts and Kenza on the Wednesday night. The show 'Don't Blush Girls' ran for almost seven years, throughout all the bombing and shelling.

Four years later, Don was surprised and delighted when Peanuts and Kenza suddenly paid him a visit. They were both dressed in military uniform, having been employed with an American Army Entertainment Unit. They had made time to see Don before their return to America. Don learned that Peanuts had been recently diagnosed as having cancer of the lung and was being sent home for treatment. It was a mere three weeks later that Don received the sad news of Peanuts' death.

Don always tried to introduce a new show at the beginning of each year and the popularity of the strip-tease item became such that it had to be an integral part of all his subsequent productions. Many of his friends and colleagues did not agree, like Georgie Wood, 'You should be ashamed, Billy, putting all this strip-tease business into your shows. Where is your artistic integrity?' to which Don replied, 'Artistic integrity is a luxury which I cannot afford. On the contrary, my rule book says:

> "The drama's laws the drama's patrons give,
> And those who live to please must please to live."'

His credo served him well and soon he had five successful revues on the road simultaneously.

Gertie had decided to retire. She had always promised herself that she would do so before she reached the age of fifty. Rather than let her audiences see her grow old and no longer on top form, she wanted to bow out gracefully. After all, she had worked since she was four years old and she certainly did not need the money. When Don suggested that she might do a farewell tour she flatly refused. That was not her style, she would go quietly while she was still on top.

Gertie's going was not to be quite as quiet as she had planned. *The Daily Express* had requested an interview and Don had accepted on Gertie's behalf. She had never courted publicity and was unhappy about the whole thing but she agreed to give an interview as long as Don remained in the room.

It did not go well. The reporter was impertinent and persisted in questioning Gertie about her financial standing. 'Aren't you the richest woman in music hall? Didn't you buy your mother a pub? How much did you get for the Kilburn Empire?' On and on. Don was forced to ask him to leave. As the reporter was escorted to the door he turned to Don and said, 'There'll be no gutters for Gertie, then.' The headlines in the *Express* the following morning did nothing to reassure.

The article spoke only of Gertie's financial assets, listing everything down to the last penny, putting words into her mouth as if she had been boasting of her personal wealth. Gertie was distraught. Anyone reading that article would assume that she was a greedy, money-grubbing woman. Fortunately everyone who knew Gertie knew that was not the case and many friends called to offer support and reassurance.

As a rule Gertie never allowed what was said in the newspapers to bother her in the least, so many ridiculous stories were printed that any sane person had to laugh, but the *Express* article was beyond the pale. Even after her death it was reported that she had been the richest woman in variety and a comment which had been erroneously attributed to her, 'No Gutters For Gertie', continued to haunt Don.

In 1940, although Don had passed his Medical Fitness Examination, he was denied entrance to the services because his work in entertainment was considered to be more important than any military contribution he might make. Although he was unhappy about that decision, he concentrated on his business which was quite literally booming. Don had five shows on the road and he would sit by the telephone every Saturday night waiting for the show managers to communicate their individual reports with the final figures for the preceding week. He was constantly surprised by the increasing success of each one.

In September of 1940 Don opened a new show at the East Ham Palace. The first week went well under the careful supervision of Belle and Gertie and Don took time off on the Saturday afternoon to attend a matinee performance of D'Oyly Carte's *The Mikado* at the Golders Green Hippodrome. During the performance the air-raid warning sirens sounded, quickly followed by the sound of an explosion. Although everyone was warned against leaving the theatre, Don had but one thought and that was to get home to Belle and Gertie.

Running the short distance home Don found the two women waiting for him. Tea and sandwiches had been prepared and the car was ready to take them all to the theatre for that evening's performance. Then the telephone rang. The manager from the East Ham Palace informed Don that the roof of the Palace was ablaze. As many of the props as could be gathered together had already been placed in the car park and all artistes were making there own way home. There was no point in his going to the theatre that night.

The following morning there was another call from the theatre manager. Three of the show's artistes were missing, Michael, Hero and Bobby Olrac. The wardens were sure that they were in one of the London hospitals. In any case there was nothing to be done but wait for news of them.

When, after two days, there was still no news of the missing artistes Don was asked to go the Manor Park mortuary to view the bodies awaiting identification. He set out, bravely, accompanied by his theatre manager, one of the comedians from the show and a flask of brandy.

On the way the sirens sounded and they were obliged to take shelter. After the all clear sounded Don's companions decided they had had enough for one day and, unable to face the ordeal ahead, left him to complete the grisly task alone.

In the cold empty ante room of the mortuary Don calmed himself with a quick slug of brandy. 'I did not know what to expect and I didn't want to behave badly.'

A young soldier came out of the inner room and passed Don on his way out. The porter shook his head sadly, 'Poor devil, twenty years old. He's just identified nine bodies. Dad, mother, sisters, brothers, grandma and his sweetheart. All found in the Anderson shelter at the bottom of their garden. Direct hit.'

The siren sounded again. Don was informed that there were no shelters; after all there was little use for them in a mortuary! As the sounds of planes and shelling became uncomfortably close the porter showed Don a refuge, a newly dug grave. After removing the covering boards Don descended the ladder into the cold and murky depths of the grave.

As he waited for the raid to pass he was glad of his flask of brandy and even managed a laugh as he entertained the macabre thought of a new corpse arriving to occupy the site and crying, 'Who's been sleeping in *my* grave?' At least if he did receive a direct hit they would not have to move his body far.

But the cruel, sobering reality of the situation was soon brought home to him when he had to face the difficult task of identifying the bodies of his friends.

The room was full of racks, like shelves in an oven. All I could see were rows and rows of bare feet. The place smelled strange. The porter pulled the racks out, one at a time, revealing bodies of all shapes and sizes covered in rough sacking. Their faces were a hideous beetroot colour. 'Caused by the blast,' the porter explained. 'Bursts their lungs.'

Unable to identify any of the bodies, Don hastily returned to his office in Shaftesbury Avenue.

News of Michael eventually filtered through. He was in hospital, having sustained fractures to both arms and legs in that raid. He was able to tell the story of how he, his wife, Hero and Bobby Olrac had sheltered in the basement of a shop in East Ham High Street when the air-raid alarm had sounded. A huge explosion had wrecked the building, which collapsed on top of them. Michael was pinned down by a girder as his wife and Bobby disappeared under falling masonry.

The next day Don had to return to the mortuary where he was able to identify the remains of Hero. All that was left of poor Bobby was his thick bush of black curly hair. Choking back the tears, Don hurried away.

CHAPTER 7

CIRCUS LIFE

When Don suddenly announced his latest idea Gertie was more than a little taken aback. What did he know about the circus? 'It's something I've always wanted to do. I've seen plenty. I may not know how they do it but I certainly know what I expect to see in a circus programme. Its arrangement and balance isn't so different from the other types of show I have done. The ingredients are different that's all.'

'Where do you get the acts?' Belle enquired, 'animals and equipment?'

Don was certain that this would be relatively easy. Even though there was a war on there were still some family circuses on the road, one-pole tent shows. Gertie was horrified at the thought of Don tenting, but he was confident that he could get a good show together as he had always done in the past. At first he would use what good circus acts he could find and introduce them to music hall. Tenting would come later.

Gertie remained sceptical but the more Don thought about it the more the circus idea appealed to him. Ever since his first visit to a circus as a child he had wanted to be a part of it. Not just a part of the show, the excitement generated by unusual acts and exotic animals, but to be involved with the 'behind scenes' activity. The organisation and management of a great circus was as equally fascinating and had long been a secret dream, which was about to be realised.

Determined to make a success of his new venture Don spent an entire summer following circus routes around Britain. Because many of the performers were one day stands it was always difficult to keep track of them. Even more difficult was the problem of keeping up with the circuses themselves. Circus proprietors kept their movements secret, which seems to be defeating their purpose somewhat because, if a show is not advertised, how can the audiences appear? The practice was intended to keep rival circuses in the dark and even the performers were not told about their next site more than a day or two in advance. It was a cut-throat business and it was not unknown for a rival firm to reach a site ahead of the booked show and set up their own tent first.

Once the summer season had ended most circus people were disengaged and desperately looking for jobs, especially those who faced the problem of animals to feed and shelter. Don was able to take his pick of the talented polished acts which would appear successfully on a music hall bill, but the majority were family acts, many with animals such as performing dogs or monkeys: acts which were suitable for a circus bill but not quite up to standard for a music hall act.

Nevertheless, Don's eye for talent singled out some exceptional acts, like the Sandows with their performing Shetland ponies, including a talking pony who was able to select handkerchiefs by colour at the behest of the audience.

Tom Fossett, together with his wife and nephew, performed a spectacular riding act, but their main asset was a little monkey called Mae West. This little character would be dressed in the style of her counterpart with a sequin-spangled dress, ostrich-feathered hat and dainty little parasol. The image was completed by liberal daubs of rouge and lipstick. If the make-up was not applied to little Mae West's satisfaction she would cling to the quarter pole and scream her displeasure until the matter was rectified by Mrs Fossett.

Once ready to 'go on', the monkey performed a tight rope walk. At first she would behave coyly, refusing to have anything to do with the vulgar display. Eventually she would allow herself to be persuaded to walk the rope, seizing the ringmaster's top hat in the process. The audience loved every minute of the performance as she ran back and forth along the rope with the top hat, always just out of reach of the ring master. A true prima donna, she would only ever allow Tom Fossett or his wife to pet or handle her, everyone else was treated with the utmost disdain.

There were many circus acts which used animals of all breeds and sizes but Don soon discovered that children liked the small animals best of all. Lions, tigers, even the beautiful liberty horses were as nothing compared to the performing dogs and cats of the domestic variety.

'La Royal and Her Cats' was one extremely popular act with adults and children alike. Cats are notoriously difficult to handle at the best of times and would often 'do their own thing' in the middle of the act. La Royal knew how to keep order. Her fingernails were finely manicured and rather long, she would give a little nip to the tummy of any recalcitrant just to remind him or her that they were supposed to be performing. For the finale a carousel was brought in and, as La Royal called each cat by name, they took their place on the merry-go-round. Then calling to the orchestra, 'Mr Maestro, some nice hurry-up music, please,' as the band played fast and loud the carousel began to spin and the cats clung to their perches for dear life. The curtain came down to tremendous applause.

Circuses attract eccentric characters and Don met many of them. On one occasion, when he was visiting a small circus looking for business, he was approached by a lady named Thanya. He accepted the invitation to visit her trailer.

Thanya was still wearing the remains of yesterday's make-up and her faded golden hair sported a toque of brightly coloured stones, diamanté and sequins, everything that glittered. She wore a harem-style costume of gold tinsel material. The ankles of the voluminous trousers were cinched with bands of more glittering stones and round her waist she wore a belt of highly polished horse brasses. 'I am Thanya, Queen of the Serpents,' she announced haughtily as Don sat himself on a large trunk in the corner of the trailer. 'You realise, of course, Mr Ross, that I am a lady and do this work only as a hobby. Did you see my performance?' Don had to admit that he had not. 'A small show like this is hardly my métier, Mr Ross. I have worked the best halls in the world.' Then, looking out of the window and gesturing to the one pole tent, 'This is not my class, really.'

Don looked at her, sitting regally in her chair, like a queen on her throne. 'Madame Thanya,' he replied, 'working in this show must suit you. I don't like to hear artistes running down the people for whom they work.'

Thanya continued unabashed, 'Please don't misunderstand me, Mr Ross. They are very nice people to work for. But we've decided not to go abroad this year; we'd much prefer to come with your show. I have five large pythons and a splendid wardrobe.'

It was not until Thanya asked Don to stand up so she could check that her snakes were all right that he realised, to his horror, he had been sitting on the chest which housed them.

Thanya's act was more showmanship than anything else, lasting only five or six minutes, as she danced with several huge reptiles wrapped around her. They must have been extremely heavy but easy to handle as long as they were fed. The pythons stole most of the limelight because of their novelty value.

The snakes were fed once a month and it was only when they were hungry that they became lively. On one occasion one of the pythons, obviously feeling peckish, took a bite at Thanya's bottom. When she hurriedly dropped the thing it started racing round the circus ring at an alarming pace. As the audience in the front row began to vacate their seats Thanya's husband had the presence of mind to throw a sack over it so it could be safely returned to its box.

Don soon acquired a selection of good acts on his book and was ready to open his first theatre circus. It was on 7th December 1942 and Don chose the Savoy Theatre in Scunthorpe in which to open for an anticipated run of fifteen weeks. This was a tactical decision on his part. A new venture needed a modest beginning; if it failed, then not too many people would hear about it if it was hidden away in the sticks. Since the name of Don Ross had begun to acquire a reputation with the professionals and public alike, he could not afford to fall flat on his face.

Gertie and Belle were there for the opening as usual, to give moral support as well as trying to soothe Don's strained nerves. Anxious as always when putting on a new show, Don went to the theatre early, alone. Belle and Gertie were to attend the second house.

Don need not have worried, the show was an instant success and the run was extended for many months. Theatre managers were clamouring for Don's circus, he already had many good acts lined up and within four weeks had another circus on the road.

One of the oldest circus families in the world, Chipperfield, were unable to continue their circus business during the war years because the younger men were all in the services. Richard and Marjorie Chipperfield joined Don, bringing with them a magnificent team of Liberty horses. Don also booked other animal acts such as black bears and Bengal tigers. Although today the use of wild animals in such presentations is deplored, the animal acts were then as much a part of the circus as the traditional clowns. Without them it could not be called circus.

Animals take a great deal of looking after and are expensive to transport and feed. Even the management of everyday animals such as horses posed problems. Since the advent of the horseless carriage stabling could be difficult to come by. Whenever an air raid occurred it was enough to send any animal crazy with fear and necessitated the owners and helpers sitting by their cages, often for the duration of the night. They tried to calm and reassure the frightened beasts by talking to them in soft voices.

The enchanting atmosphere of circus life has always attracted youths wishing to be a part of it all. One such young hopeful was a twelve-year-old by the name of William Jefferson. He was allowed to help with odd jobs and given a small remuneration. Although it was forbidden for any of the young helpers to be in the vicinity of the caged animals, William got too close to a bear's cage one day and almost had his arm torn off. He was saved by one of the performing dogs who jumped through the bars of the cage and bit the bear's leg until it let go of the boy. After extensive surgery to save the arm and thirteen weeks in hospital, young William was restored to health. Sadly, only a few years later Don learned that William Jefferson had been run over and killed by a bus.

Theatre managers were pressing Don for more circus dates. Christmas and holiday periods were those most sought after and before long a third circus was launched. Don had a monopoly on stage circuses and 'Don Ross's Royal Imperial Circus' was soon working every theatre and music hall in Great Britain. All in all, Don had certainly found another success with his circuses and, together with five revues already on the road and weekly variety shows, business was booming.

It seemed inevitable that Don's next step should be 'tenting'. Tom Fossett was the first to suggest it. After three years of indoor work he was itching to feel the grass under his feet once more. Of course it was not in Don's nature to refuse any reasonable suggestion and he was eager to give it a try, although he was aware of the difficulties and extra costs that such an operation was likely to entail.

As Don was discussing the extra equipment needed with Tom, he happened to mention that he and his wife would need a trailer. Don was surprised because the Fossetts already had a large vehicle on a site at Towcester. On enquiring about this, Tom Fossett lowered his voice before explaining that the vehicle in question was full of money! Never having believed in banks, the Fossetts' entire life savings were in that van. Full of gold and silver coins, it was immovable.

Don always respected the feelings, ideas and superstitions of the circus folk. Wanting to be part of every aspect of the show, Don would ask to be shown and instructed on any detail which was new to him. Invariably the reply would be, 'Guv'nor, you've got your hands full running the business side of the show. Leave everything else to us.' They were not prepared to divulge what might seem trivial matters to an outsider. Such things were their professional secrets and Don accepted that need for privacy.

During the war years Kent and the surrounding area had been closed to them. Now that it was beginning to open up again, Tom Fossett reckoned that the public should be ready for some light entertainment.

Following Tom's advice Don arranged for their circus to open at Redhill, Surrey. After three days there they made their way to Reigate. Don was discovering exactly how hard a life tenting could be, a twenty-four hours a day job with no time allowed for relaxation. Even after the evening show, however tired one might be, sleep was interrupted by the slightest change in the weather. Ever listening for the flapping of the big top in case a breeze blew up. Always expecting a call from the tentmaster to tighten or loosen, or if a calamity was expected to lower it altogether. During waking hours general maintenance, painting and cleaning kept everyone busy. Battling against the vagaries of the weather and continual travelling it was a major effort to keep everything looking smart.

Although there was a regular staff of grooms and attendants, extra help was occasionally required. This necessitated the hiring of casual workers picked-up along the way. Many strange characters came and went and often pieces of equipment and uniforms would go with them.

Petrol was still rationed so careful route planning was essential in order to get the most out of the allowances. Don always tried to keep travelling distance between stops to twenty miles and arrange for a stay of one week in the larger resorts which always meant good business. But there were occasions when they had to set up the big top in the nearest village.

Although it was hard work and it cannot be said that anyone, however dedicated, could love every minute of such a life on the road, Don did find certain aspects of it exciting. He loved to watch the public as they made their way to the pay boxes. This sight always gave him a thrill and on occasion he could not resist the temptation to become totally involved as he stood outside and called 'Walk up, walk up!' Tom Fossett was not amused, considering it to be beneath Don's status to be out front like that. Don replied, 'Mr Tom, ever since I was a small boy I've longed to stand outside a circus tent and shout, "Walk up, walk up". Now that I actually own one, nobody's going to stop me.' Then, after a pause, 'But I promise I won't do it too often and disgrace you.'

Moving days meant rising at five in the morning. One of the show women would bring Don a cup of tea, followed a few minutes later by another, then another until several cups of tea were lined up on the dresser. It was circus tea, hot, strong and very sweet. For Don it was undrinkable, but he never allowed the kind tea ladies to find out that it all went down the drain.

Moving was always a major operation and, if the weather was against them, heavy ground sodden with rain made it extremely difficult to get the vans moving at all. The lorry which carried the canvas tent poles and tent men would lead the way, immediately followed by Don's caravan. Everyone else made their own way in their own time, the last one making sure that the ground was left clean and tidy. Obviously there were some who would be delayed so, when the leading lorry came to a fork in the road, Don would dismount, gather a clutch of greenery from the hedgerow and place it in the middle of the road they had taken. This was apparently an old gypsy custom.

As soon as the advance party arrived at the new site the tent canvas would be spread out, the king poles situated in position before lacing. Finally, the top was erected. By that time the kitchen wagon would be ready to produce a king-sized breakfast for the workers.

As soon as the animals arrived on site they had to be fed and watered. Animals always took precedence over people and by the time they were accommodated it was time for the first show to commence, so their grooms and handlers had to wait for their meal.

It was a successful season and as it was about to draw to a close Don was already planning his winter tour of the halls. He needed a strong six-minute act to fill a vacant spot, something quite special. As if in answer to a prayer a young woman fire-eater presented herself.

Don noticed that she was far from beautiful and shabbily dressed; nevertheless the poor lighting needed for a fire-eating act would hide her lack of physical attributes and she must have some good stage costumes. Without seeing her perform Don arranged for a night at Collins Music Hall in Islington. Donna Delbert, for that was her stage name, performed very well and Don engaged her for further appearances.

The audiences liked Miss Delbert's act, so did Don, but although he could not put his finger on it, he had a strange feeling that something was not quite right about the lady. It was not until she visited Don at his office some time later that he realised what it was. Donna Delbert was a man. This explained the face without a trace of make-up, even on stage, plus the fact that he had extremely large hands and feet. When Don faced Delbert with this discovery he left the office very quickly without any explanation. He still had several dates booked and it was some weeks later that Don heard that Donna Delbert had been arrested by the United States Air Force Officials for desertion. He was found guilty by court martial and sentenced to two years' hard labour. That was the end of Donna Delbert's short but successful stage career.

As the winter season was nearing its close Don was offered what seemed like a wonderful proposition, a full summer season at Margate. It was an offer not to be refused as it meant three full months' business without any touring. Don had just signed the contract to open in Margate at the end of June 1946 when the agent, Nat Day, phoned. 'Where are you on June 10th?' When Don explained that he would be in Margate Nat insisted that he should put it back a week, 'I want you for the Peace Celebrations at the Empire Pool, Wembley, and the money will be good.' It was a wonderful offer, not just for the money, but for the prestige which would accompany such a booking.

Don could not wait to get started but as soon as he saw the huge Empire Pool his heart almost stopped. The sheer size of the place was overwhelming. A one-ring circus would look ridiculous in such a venue, it had to be a three-ring or nothing.

The idea was novel, he would be the first promoter ever to stage a three-ring circus in Britain. It also meant that many more performers would have to be engaged to fill those three rings. This was where Don's previous hard work served him in good stead and he was able to collect some of the best circus acts of the day. When his final programme was completed he sent it to the Ministry of Works who were the actual employers. They were more than satisfied with the arrangements that Don had suggested and in reply offered him an extra £250 over and above the original contracted fee.

It was a huge operation and truly fitting of the official Peace Celebrations. Each day eight thousand children were brought by special trains and buses from all areas of London to attend the performances at 10.30 a.m and 2.30 p.m.

Despite all his careful preparations Don suffered his usual attack of first night nerves. He was convinced that his starting signal, a short blast on a whistle, would go unheeded. Again, there was no need for him to worry. As soon as Don blew the whistle, as if by magic, the Empire Pool became a mass of activity. From each of the six entrances participants in a great wild west show invaded the scene. Cowboys, cowgirls, horses, rope spinners and knife and axe throwers got the show off to an exciting start. It was pure spectacle which was increased three fold as the three rings were simultaneously occupied and kept up a fast pace throughout the entire show.

The finale was no less spectacular. More than eighty stilt walkers paraded in carnival costumes, together with the two hundred artistes who had appeared in the show. Belle Fossett, dressed as Britannia and riding a white horse, entered the centre ring and mounting the steps rode to the top of the rostrum. Once she and her horse were in position a soloist sang, 'Land of Hope and Glory'. The company and audience joined in the choruses.

It was a great finish to one of Don's greatest achievements to date. But if he felt any self satisfaction about that great event it was to be short lived. The gods had decided that they had smiled on him too kindly of late, Margate was already threatening to become a fiasco. Don was to remember it as, 'The unhappiest, most uncomfortable and unpleasant engagement I ever worked in my life.'

As he and Gertie motored to the site Don noted with dismay that the posters advertising the event were of exceedingly poor quality. Circus posters, as everyone surely knows, are always huge and printed in bright multi-colours, brash and instant, meant to catch the eye and convey the very spirit of the circus. The posters that Don saw were hardly visible because they bore a pale mauve print which was almost lost on a yellow background. This was a flagrant breach of the conditions of his contract with the Margate management.

Don had spent four years of hard work making his circuses the most notable in the country, he now discovered that his name did not even appear on the bill matter. The Margate managers had taken it upon themselves to change the name of Don's circus to 'Casino Continental Circus'. Understandably, he was furious, and if it had not been for the fact that he had already engaged fifty performers, together with a large selection of animals and grooms and circus attendants all dependent on the work, he would have walked out there and then.

To make matters worse Don discovered that the lighting for the show was not being provided by the local authority but by the management's own dynamos. Don knew from past experience that this meant potential disaster and he always demanded that the local electricity board ran a cable from the mains to ensure a satisfactory supply. It was too late to do anything about the arrangement for that night's performance and Don was forced to accept the situation.

The first half of the show went well. It was a full house and the audience was appreciative. The second half started well, then Don's worst fears were realised as the lighting began to fail just as the 'Sensational Carsons', a sharp-shooting and knife-throwing act, were about to enter the ring. It could not have happened at a worse time. Jack Carson refused to go on with the act and Don would never have expected him to. He gave word to Tom Fossett to cut and go straight to the finale. By this time the audience could barely see what was going on and Don was forced to let them leave with a poor opinion of what was in fact a first-rate show.

By this time Don was distraught but, determined to remain calm, come what may, he said nothing to the Margate organisers about the debacle.

The next evening he noticed that someone was employed in painting the inside of the ring fence using the same insipid mauve and yellow that had been used on the posters. Don explained to the woman, who turned out to be a relative of the managers, that this area must remain white, it was a guide for the horses to follow, it had to be so. The woman ignored him and this led to an exchange of words, with her husband joining in.

Returning to his living quarters Don was thankful that Gertie was there to calm and soothe. What should have been another great success was fast becoming a nightmare. It was all the more galling after their stupendous success at Wembley. It had taken Don many years to build himself a reputation in this business and now it looked as if that reputation was about to be destroyed in a single week, if the show could last that long.

Gertie would not allow that to happen and insisted that they should contact the head of the Margate management before any more damage was done. After a search the appropriate person was found in a local dance hall. Gertie, all five feet one inch of her, strode across the floor and told this person exactly what she thought of him. She concluded by stating that they would be leaving the very next morning, artistes, animals, the lot. If Margate wanted a circus they had better start looking for one.

Before the evening was out Don and Gertie were visited by two of the directors, apologising profusely and promising to rectify every wrong on their part. Of course the threat to pick up and leave was all bravado. Don was fully committed to his artistes and staff whom he had already booked for the season, whatever happened, they had no choice but to stay.

Despite the promises matters did not improve. Don was ill with frustrated anger and his treatment at the hands of a bunch of amateurs. He and Gertie returned to London leaving Don's manager in charge.

Although he had to get away from the turmoil, unable to watch his hard work come to nothing, Don did not abandon the project altogether; once or twice he visited the site and found the performers working hard to salvage the show.

It was on one of those visits that Don found Tom Fossett selling photographs of his monkey, Mae West. This was perfectly acceptable as he had a clause in his contract allowing him to do so, but Don was intrigued by his patter. 'Photographs of Mae West, the wonder monkey, only threepence each. All the money goes to charity.' Then he would mumble a few more inaudible words. When Don asked about this Tom replied, 'Actually, guv'nor, I don't give any money to charity, but I keep things right with my conscience by saying to myself, "When I've done with it".'

This practice gave Thanya an idea and she started selling pieces of snake skin, claiming it to be lucky, even an alternative remedy to many common ailments.

During the last week of the circus in Margate Don and Gertie were returning home after a visit to the theatre when a fierce gale blew up. Branches were being ripped off trees in Finchley and Don's heart sank as he wondered what it would be doing to the big top in Margate. As soon as they reached home the telephone rang. It was Don's manager in Margate. The news was dire. The tent was blown to ribbons, the horses had stampeded, the monkeys had taken to the trees, the lions were terrified and one of the king poles had blown down, damaging some of the living wagons. The man was calling from a public call box because all the lines were down on the site. Everything was in chaos, it was the end. As far as Don was concerned it was a fitting end to the shambles which had preceded it. He vowed never to accept another engagement under any other management but his own.

Within three weeks Don was back with his circuses in the theatres. The following nine months were booked solid. A second circus was about to open for a four-month tour and a third was booked over the Christmas and New Year season. In the office the circuses were identified by naming them red, white or blue.

As soon as the war ended Bertram Mills lost no time with their plans to reform. Chipperfield's were also busy organising their come-back. A newcomer was also entering the competition in the form of Billy Smart. Don was vice-president of the Circus Proprietors' Association and wondered how they would all fare as they each claimed that their particular circus would be the greatest ever. Don knew to his cost the pitfalls of going on the road. Quite apart from anything else, the cost of taking out a super circus was astronomical. Someone had to fail. It resulted in a vicious war between the big boys. Don divorced himself from it. He had made money during his tenting and theatre circus productions, money that was safely in the bank. It was time to move on. Another project for Don Ross.

That was the end of Don's circus days but a sad reminder of the circus life and circus folk came in the form of a newspaper headline, 'Man Buried Alive at Garden Fête!' The man had been engaged as the main attraction of the Fête in Hertfordshire. He had been sealed in a coffin and buried in a grave beneath six feet of earth. He had claimed that after a certain time had elapsed he would be brought out unharmed. Tragically, when the coffin was opened the man was dead. The man turned out to be the husband of Thanya, Queen of the Snakes. It was not long after that Don heard of Thanya's death. She had been found dead in her caravan.

CHAPTER 8

THANKS FOR THE MEMORY

One evening, after a visit to the theatre, Belle and Gertie were enjoying a cup of tea and Don a glass of whisky when Gertie broke the silence, ' What's on your mind, darling?' She always knew when Don might be cooking up a new project. 'You've got a thoughtful look on your face.'

'You know that I've had the idea in mind for a nostalgic type of show. I think now is the time to do it. I even have the title, "Thanks for the Memory".' Gertie looked at him, teapot poised in mid-stream. Belle sat up. They waited for Don to continue.

'I think if I could get George Elliott, Nellie Wallace, Hettie King and Lily Morris to start off with . . .'

'Oh, that sounds wonderful.' Gertie could not hide her enthusiasm. 'I wouldn't mind taking part in it myself.'

Don liked the idea. 'Do you really mean that? It would be great, Gertie. You've been off the stage for nigh on ten years, which would make your appearance all the more exciting. What do you think, Belle?'

Belle took a little time to reply. 'If Gertie feels like doing it, well and good. Remember, she hasn't sung a note in all that time. She needs to find out what her voice sounds like now. She would also have to get busy practising her tap dancing and saxophone playing.' It appeared that Belle was pouring cold water on the idea but her comments were valid. Gertie had not made a stage appearance for ten years, a long time to be out of harness for any professional. Belle did not want to see her fall flat. Gertie, however, was not to be put off and her thoughts raced ahead. 'I've no intention of letting you tour without me. The office can keep

93

going for a while and we'll be in touch by telephone, every day.' Gertie had made up her mind, there was no stopping her now. 'Wherever we go I want the best suite in the best hotels and the car with our own chauffeur, Harry, to tour with us.'

It was Don's turn to be taken aback. 'That was quite a speech, darling. You worked that lot out pretty quickly. I seem to remember some years ago, when Tom Arnold asked you to appear in his show, "The Stars That Made Variety", you refused. You insisted that you did not intend to work again and even if you did it would not be with a veteran show!'

Gertie merely smiled as she poured herself another cup of tea.

It also came as a surprise to Don that Gertie insisted on staying in the best hotels. During her working life she had always stayed in theatrical digs, as did her colleagues. Belle O'Connor had kept a book listing all the digs throughout the country which in her opinion were the best. She also saw to it that Gertie was accommodated in the most comfortable rooms with the best landladies.

It was now past midnight but the adrenaline was flowing. Unable to wait until morning, Don cabled George Elliott, who was on holiday in Lucerne. It was 28th August 1947, his cable read,

Thinking of taking out a show called 'Thanks for the Memory'. Suggested cast Gertie, Nellie Wallace, Hetty King, Lily Morris. To commence immediately after pantomime. Would you like to come with us?

George's reply came the following afternoon. He would be delighted to join the show. The rest of the cast was not quite so easy to engage. Don did not know it at the time but Nellie Wallace and Lily Morris had some sort of feud going on between them. Neither could be persuaded to appear on the same bill. Both were friends of Don and Gertie and the situation could have been embarrassing for all concerned, but Lily Morris decided not to accept Don's offer. She was fully retired now and did not want to tour again. She thanked Don for contacting her and wished him the best for the success of his show. Gertie and Don had to try hard to conceal their relief.

Nellie was concerned that it was going to be a veteran show, 'bath chairs at the stage door, and all that'. Don assured her that it would not be billed as such but no-one could prevent the press and others from making such allegations. Nellie was not the easiest woman in the world to do business with but she was a great comedienne, Don regarded her as one of the all-time greats and he wanted her in his show at any price, so he agreed via her daughter, Norah, who was also Nellie's manager, to an above average salary if she could persuade her mother to appear with them on tour.

Once Don was sure of his cast for the show he drew up the bill, contacted the head booker for the Moss Empire circuit and offered his proposition. Before the morning was out another important booker contacted Don. The grapevine was working well, she had heard about Don's show and had just three things to say: 'Was it true? Was Gertie going to be in it? If so promise to open at the Empress Theatre, Brixton, the ideal theatre for that type of show.' Don agreed and gave his word that, come what may, they would open at the Empress. After all, Brixton was the home of the 'pros'. At least sixty per cent of them came from or lived in Brixton.

When Don showed the booker for Moss Empires, Cissie Williams, his bill she was delighted and contacted Val Parnell, whose immediate reaction was, 'This will be one of the biggest sensations we've had in this business for years. We must have two weeks in each hall all round the tour. We've a smash hit on our hands.'

It was just what Don had wanted to hear. He was already convinced of the show's potential but it was good to know that others shared his enthusiasm.

When Val had left the office Cissie opened the ledger of bookings and commenced to fill in the dates. Don interrupted with, 'I want one week at each hall, not two. I'd sooner have one big slap bang sell-out week than spread the business over two weeks.' Cissie did not agree but Don insisted and he also insisted that they should open at the Empress, Brixton, to honour his promise. Cissie called him a fool. 'If they wanted to get rid of you they wouldn't hesitate, you know.'

As Don left the office with a year's work already booked Cissie called to him, 'I wish you all the luck in the world but you know that you have the two most difficult people that this business has ever had to deal with. Talbot O'Farrell and

Nellie Wallace. If you can control those two for three months, you're a better man than I'd give you credit for!'

When Don approached Hetty King about the show he was disappointed. She demanded £175 a week, plus top billing, number one dressing room and she reserved the right to choose whomsoever she wished to work with, eliminating all those she did not like, and finally she must be allowed to choose her own spot on the programme. Don, refusing to have his hands tied thus, bade her goodnight.

Ella Shields was the next name which came to mind, although Don did not know how to contact her. Georgie Wood solved the problem. 'Cable her care of Bank of Australia, Brisbane. They will contact her, but don't ask her what salary she wants because if you do, dear Ella will open her mouth so wide she'll queer it for herself. Tell her what you're prepared to pay.'

Don thanked Georgie who also wanted to be in the show but Don had to say no. This show was essentially nostalgia, those well-loved songs that various artistes had made their own. Georgie's act was not in keeping with the spirit of what Don had in mind. Georgie was an old friend so it was especially difficult to refuse him but there were no hard feelings.

On 8th September Don cabled Ella Shields:

Offer engagement with 'Thanks for the Memory'. Featuring George, Gertie, Nellie and others commencing end of February. Already booked complete Moss and Stoll tours. Salary £100.
Kind regards, Don Ross.

Two days later Don had his reply. Ella's season did not end until January and she requested to join the show in March. Don replied that her contract was in the post and they were due to open 23rd February at the Brixton Empress. Ella cabled back that she would be proud to appear in such distinguished company.

Don's new show was soon the talk of the town. Everyone knew about it and everyone wanted to be in it. Randolph Sutton telephoned, 'Is there a spot for me in your new show?' Don protested. He had never thought of Randolph as an old timer. Randolph insisted that he was as old as any of the others appearing on the bill, he just made it to the top a little later than them. Don agreed and Randolph

Sutton's name was added to the list.

As soon as George Elliott returned from Switzerland he paid Don and Gertie a visit. He was bubbling over with enthusiasm at the thought of working with Don and Gertie again. There was so much to discuss. First of all the question of billing had to be dealt with. George suggested that they should follow their old practice and he and Gertie should share top billing. That was acceptable to all concerned. Before long the old friends had slipped back into their customary chat as if they had never been apart.

The only possible problem that Don could foresee was Nellie Wallace. She could be difficult at the best of times and Don knew that it would require every ounce of diplomacy that he could summon if the matter of Nellie's contract was to be settled amicably.

When Don telephoned her she hemmed and hawed, refusing to give a definite answer. Nellie's daughter, Norah, was probably the only person who could handle her and she invited Don and Gertie to dinner the following Sunday. She guaranteed that her mother would sign.

They enjoyed a splendid meal at Nellie's beautiful home in Bryanstone Court and after dinner Don tentatively broached the subject of the contract. 'I need it signed, Nellie. What about it?'

Nellie put on her 'looking into space' expression as if she had not heard a word that Don had said. 'Come on, Nellie dear, here's a pen.' Don offered his pen.

'I don't know that I am going to sign it,' Nellie said airily. Norah lost her patience then. She had already spent hours discussing the matter with her mother who had been enthusiastic about the tour; at that time. After Norah's tirade Nellie laughed and signed the contract. 'Gave you a bit of a run-around then, didn't I?'

Don pocketed the precious paper. 'Not really, Nellie. I know you like a bit of a joke.'

That stalling had pleased Nellie, who was in many respects like a mischievous child. Don knew her moods only too well, at least he now had the contract and the rest of the evening could be enjoyed.

During the course of the conversation which followed Don discovered that Norah's health had been poor of late. He advised her to see a specialist.

A day or so later, as Don was congratulating himself on having overcome the most difficult problem that he could have perceived, he received a telephone call from Norah. 'May we come over right away? It's urgent.' Don's heart sank as he feared the worst. The contract might have been signed but Nellie was going to start creating difficulties. He was wrong, the problem was not of Nellie's making.

When they arrived Don was surprised to see Norah dressed in a housecoat. Gertie sensed the seriousness of Norah's visit and suggested that Belle and Nellie might take a walk round the garden before tea.

As soon as the three were alone Norah explained that she had been to see a specialist and the prognosis was not good. She was to be admitted to University College Hospital the very next day for a major operation and she wanted Don and Gertie to invite Nellie to stay with them. Alone in her own house she would have little else to do but worry. Gertie agreed at once and offered to make the suggestion to Nellie herself, in a casual off-hand manner. Nellie seemed to like the idea and, although she was frantically worried about Norah, Gertie made sure that she was at least kept occupied and befriended. Plans for the show continued apace, then, Don received a letter from George Elliott.

Dear Billy,

re: 'Thanks for the Memory'

I am writing regarding one or two points about the above show.

I worked hard during the war and have proved that I am now attracting the younger members of the public as well as many of the older folk. I am now considered quite a radio star, having done quite a lot of broadcasting of recent years. I have a big fan mail from young people and I enclose two or three letters of recent date. A show has its disadvantages, you usually have a finale. In variety it only happens occasionally. With a show you do a long run of weeks without a rest and in these days of high taxation it means most of your money goes to the state. In variety one like myself can arrange two or three weeks then rest a week or two. One can take things more restfully and still come out of it financially not too bad.

I myself am not happy over this show, so think it better for all concerned if I stay out of it. You see, Billy, when I first received your telegram in Lucerne being on holiday I did not give it my full consideration and naturally wired back 'yes' on the spur of the moment. But having time to think it over, I now look at the suggestion in a different light. Any publicity that has already gone out regarding the show can be overcome by stating that owing to other contracts and commitments already entered into prevented me appearing in the show. There is no need for this to cause offence either side as it is purely a business proposition.

Best love and wishes to Gertie, Mrs O'Connor and yourself,

from June and yours sincerely, George.

George wanted the best of both worlds. It was a devastating blow to Don's plans and George must have realised this as he penned the letter. Don's reply was short and to the point:

I have received your intimation that you wish to withdraw from the cast of 'Thanks for the Memory'. Surely this is not the case?

You have every right to turn down an offer that does not appeal to you, but having accepted this offer by telegram and letter and having discussed with us billing and various ideas of production you are the last man in the business I would have thought would go back on your word, especially when you must realise that acting on your definite acceptance we engaged the rest of the cast and are now in the unenviable position of being forced to carry through a project which we would not have contemplated had we any idea you would be the one to let me down.

Kind regards, Billy.

This brought George to heel but he demanded top billing at all times and the number one dressing room in every theatre. He knew it was too late in the day for argument and it must have been hard for Gertie to realise that someone she had always regarded as a dear friend could behave in such a manner. For herself she did not care which particular dressing room or spot on the bill she might be allocated and she gave in to all George's whims. But she did insist that Nellie must have number two dressing room and Ella number three. Gertie would take the fourth.

Upsetting as this contretemps had been, Don refused to believe that George was solely responsible. The letter had been in his handwriting but someone else had persuaded him to write it. Don was convinced of that.

At last the final arrangements were completed. The six featured artistes had all signed their contracts. Don had exhorted them to read the wording carefully, especially the clauses relating to billing and advertising. Each artiste was informed exactly on how they would be billed, which spot they would occupy as well as the dressing room arrangements. One especially important point as far as Don was concerned was the ruling that on no account was any artiste to make a speech at the end of their act. If one did it another was bound to follow suit. It was an unnecessary waste of time and would slow down the pace of the show. Everyone was happy to comply with Don's terms and conditions.

There was still unhappiness to be faced. Norah had her operation. Don and Gertie visited her every day. She was in constant pain. Don tried to be positive, 'Maybe tomorrow will be better, love. You're bound to have a lot of discomfort after such a big operation.'

Norah knew better. 'Don't let's have any pretence. I won't be better tomorrow or the next day. The surgeon and specialist have told me, I've got six months, no longer. I am a dying woman.'

Overcome with emotion Don assured Norah that she was indeed 'a brave woman'. Promising to look after Nellie and protect her from the full agony of Norah's illness, Don and Gertie left the hospital. Eventually, Norah was allowed to return to her own home in the care of a full-time nurse.

Time was passing and the opening of 'Thanks for the Memory' drew near. For once there were no foreseeable shadows on the horizon, until Don visited the Empress, Brixton, with some advance matter. In the bar he saw a poster advertising Max Miller and included in the supporting artistes was Talbot O'Farrell. It was another body blow and Don contacted Talbot immediately. What did he think he was playing at, appearing on Max's bill three weeks before the opening of Don's show?

Don was understandably furious. There was no way that Talbot could appear at the Empress so close to the opening of 'Thanks for the Memory'. Don had the prior contract and he informed Talbot that he would have to join the show at Liverpool the following week. Billy Danvers was engaged to fill O'Farrell's spot at the Empress.

Don's next task was the happy one of welcoming Ella Shields on her return from Australia. Armed with a huge bouquet he met the boat train at St Pancras before taking her to her hotel. Don and Gertie gave a party that night to celebrate Ella's homecoming.

CHAPTER 9

CURTAIN RISE

The 23rd February 1948. At last they were ready to open. All the trials that Don had suffered in the planning for this day were forgotten. Nothing could stop them now.

In buoyant mood Don arrived at the Empress early to meet the manager, Doyle Crossley. The buoyant mood was short lived when he was informed that the gallery would have to be closed. There was a wide crack in the gallery facade, possibly caused by delayed action from the recent air raids. The manager was also depressed by the news because he had expected to break all box-office records with Don's show.

Don remained philosophical. It could have been worse, they might have closed the entire theatre. The weather could have been better, freezing fog delayed the arrival of the cast for rehearsals. Eventually everyone was assembled apart from Nellie Wallace. Nevertheless Don rehearsed the chorus dancers and those other members of the cast who were ready.

Suddenly the stage entrance doors burst open and in rushed Nellie dressed in the most bizarre fashion. Over a pair of long trousers, the ends of which were tucked into fur-lined boots, she wore a luxurious mink coat, her head and shoulders covered by an old shawl. As the others motioned to welcome her she withdrew and throwing out her arms yelled, 'Don't speak to me. I don't want anyone to speak to me.'

Realising that he had a potential crisis on his hands Don proceeded carefully. 'Nellie, just a minute, please. We are going to run through the finale. It won't take ten minutes.' Grudgingly and silently she took her place in line. The rehearsal took place and continued until Don was satisfied.

Although Nellie was noted for being difficult to manage, Don had learned how to handle her and considered any effort worthwhile to retain one of the greatest comediennes ever. He remembered one occasion when Nellie was billed to appear at the Theatre Royal in Hanley. In order to keep her sweet Don had attempted to brighten her dressing room with a bunch of chrysanthemums and a carpet purloined from the stage manager's office. Nellie was not impressed, 'Who put those damn things there? If there's one thing I detest it's chrysanthemums. They smell like bad feet.' Don had to admit liability. 'And who might you be?' Nellie demanded. As soon as she realised that she was in the presence of Don Ross, Gertie's husband, Nellie's attitude changed, 'Why didn't you say so? How kind of you to put those delightful flowers there. How is Gertie?'

Although Don knew all these artistes personally as well as professionally, he never presumed to suggest how they might organise their own individual acts. They were true professionals, whom Don had idolised from his own boyhood. They knew exactly how to conduct their own performances and please their audiences. Don was simply the manager.

On that opening night Don, Gertie and Belle arrived early as always. As soon as they passed through the stage door the atmosphere was palpable. They had been very quiet in the car on the way to the theatre and now the tense atmosphere of expectation made conversation redundant. They each knew how the other felt. Don knew how Gertie felt. When Gertie was nervous she always became quiet, she was very quiet now and he took her hand and gave it a reassuring squeeze. As they walked to their dressing rooms someone would call out to them, 'Is that you, Gertie? Everything all right?' Gertie replied in the affirmative. Then Nellie came out into the passage; taking Gertie's hand she said, 'You'll be fine once you've done the first show.'

There were telegrams and flowers arriving by the minute and the call boy had his work cut out delivering all the various bouquets to their correct destinations. Don was on hot bricks worrying as usual about the public reaction on this first night of the show. Whatever praise other members of his own profession might heap upon him, it was as nothing unless the audiences agreed.

Don stood at the front of the theatre and watched the crowds roll in. He went back stage and breathed in the glorious odours of greasepaint, dust and scenery. He heard Billy Danvers arriving with Guila. Their laughter preceded them and helped to soothe Don's jangled nerves.

'Why are you looking so worried?' Billy asked. 'You're on a clear winner. As we came in we saw two charabancs unloading, one from the Isle of Wight, the other from Portsmouth. The theatre's besieged!' Don allowed himself to be convinced. It was true. This was it. This was the culmination of all the previous months of planning.

Don stood in the wings as the show opened and Ella Shields made her entrance. She had grabbed his arm so tightly it almost hurt. Ella had always been a nervous performer and tonight was especially nerve-racking for her. She had been absent from the British stage for some time and needed to be remembered. She need not have worried, the audience not only remembered her, they loved her and showed their appreciation in the usual way. Don embraced her as she left the stage, tears streaming down her face. 'I did all right, darling, didn't I?' she whispered to Don. 'You are proud of me, aren't you?' Don assured her that he was indeed proud of her and to prove it he would present her with a bottle of champagne after the second house.

It was time for Gertie to make an appearance. Don walked with her to the stage and gave her hand an extra squeeze. She burst into laughter, 'Are you pressing my hand because you think I am nervous or is it because you are?'

'Both,' was Don's curt reply. There were so many words he wished to say but a shortage of time and an excess of emotion prevented him from doing so.

They waited in the wings together for Nellie and Randolph to finish their act, a front cloth item. Behind the tabs the stage was already set for Gertie. The grand piano was there draped with her Spanish shawls.

As soon as Nellie and Randolph left the stage the orchestra played the chorus of 'Nellie Dean' and Gertie made her first stage appearance since her retirement ten years previously. If Gertie was experiencing any first night nerves she did not let it show. She had been practising her routine for weeks and no-one would have believed that she had ever been retired at all. Now in her sixth decade, Gertie sang and tapped as well as ever. Although the voice might be a little older, the timing was just as precise, the performance just as immaculate. As always she gave her audience the very best of herself and their applause reverberated throughout the theatre.

As the curtain fell at the end of that first night's second performance they congratulated each other and themselves on having put on such a show. Even in their wildest dreams, not one of them had ever dared imagine that it would have had quite so much appeal or have drawn such crowds. Everyone was overcome with emotion, so much so that Gertie could not resist whispering to Don, 'Why are they all crying? We surely couldn't have been that bad!'

That first night was not only an absolute triumph but a precursor of what was to come. The theatre manager contacted Don to say that every single ticket had been sold for the entire week. When they eventually returned home, exhausted but happy, they were still too excited to think of going to bed. They sat up discussing the thrill they had all shared on this truly memorable occasion.

The following morning *The Performer* reviewed Don's show as:

One of the greatest music hall happenings for a generation. Seldom, if ever, in its long and colourful history has the Empress witnessed such stirring scenes as those which greeted the première of Don Ross's 'Thanks for the Memory'. A company of six of our greatest music hall artistes.

After this Cissie Williams contacted Don in an effort to persuade him to think again about his insistence on one-week appearances at each of the Moss Empires.

'You'd better come over straight away, we'll have to re-adjust the whole tour. Make it two weeks in each town as Val and I suggested.'

On his arrival at Cissie's office Don was informed by a delighted Cissie that the theatre manager of the Liverpool Empire had reported that all tickets had been sold for all the appearances of 'Thanks for the Memory', which was due to open there the following week. There was a queue stretching a block or more from the theatre. People just did not believe that there were no tickets available.

'You've kept the fifth week open, haven't you?' Cissie wanted to know.

'Of course, Holy Week. We might as well have that week off. It's only five nights, that's no proposition for us.'

Cissie was adamant. 'Five nights or not you'll go back to Liverpool for that week! Now, let's sort out the rest of the tour. I'm going to prove you were wrong to insist on one-week stands.'

Cissie had spoken. There was no point in arguing, as if anyone would want to. The show promised to be an even greater success than any of them could have imagined or even hoped for.

The *News of the World* were next to contact Don. Having heard of the big hit in Brixton they wanted to photograph the artistes taking part. Don was more than pleased and welcomed the publicity. He had never employed a press agent always having considered it unnecessary, preferring the press to come to him. This way he thought that he would get better treatment and, although he was sure that was the right way to do it, nevertheless Don had to admit that on certain occasions a press agent could be an asset.

The *News of the World* gave them a big spread with photographs of all the stars involved in the show as well as an enthusiastic write-up. Whilst everyone involved was busily congratulating themselves and each other, Nellie Wallace remained on the sidelines. She was quite literally going through hell. Her only daughter, her mainstay and manager, was dying and there was nothing anyone could do to prevent it.

When Nellie started the tour with the show it would be better for Norah if she returned to hospital care. Although Norah had tried to keep the bad news from her mother for as long as possible, they both knew that once Norah returned to hospital it would be for the last time and time was running out.

It was on a Saturday afternoon that the ambulance came to take Norah away. She asked them to wait while she took one long last look at her room. At their front door Nellie kissed her daughter. 'Oh, Mother darling, it would have been better if we had been killed together in the air raids rather than finishing like this.' Nellie could not trust herself to speak. She returned to Norah's empty room where she sat quietly until the door bell rang. It was the chauffeur to take her to the theatre. Donning her coat she went to work. All she asked of her colleagues was to leave her alone, she could not trust herself to speak to any one of them.

Nellie steeled herself to go on stage and make the audiences roar with laughter as her own heart was breaking.

Although Don and Gertie tried their best to comfort Nellie, there was no point in pretending. They all knew that Norah was dying. In an effort to relieve the despair a little they invited Nellie and Ella Shields to their hotel suite on the Sunday evening for dinner. It was a difficult evening for all concerned and as soon as dinner was over Nellie returned to her room.

Early next morning Don was awakened by a furious knocking at the door of their rooms. Nellie was outside still in her night clothes and in an agitated state. She was wearing a fur coat with another draped over her right arm, a handbag on her left arm and a glass of water in her left hand.

Don invited her inside. She paced the floor refusing to sit down and insisting that she must return to London. Gertie had joined them by this time and offered some commonsense advice. 'I know how you feel, Nellie darling, but what good would it do to return to London? Forget about the show, go if you feel you must. But remember, here you are surrounded by friends who love you and, what's more important, you have your work. I know you don't need it financially but it may be the one thing that will save you.'

Nellie was emotionally drained. 'You may be right, but it won't save my Norah, will it?'

'Nothing can save your Norah.' Don had to make her face up to the situation, however cruel the words might seem, but Nellie was not listening. She insisted on returning to London. The more Don and Gertie offered their help and comfort the more Nellie resisted. Her beloved daughter was dying and she could not come to terms with it. There was nothing that either of them could ever say that would help.

Ever practical, Gertie ordered tea and advised Nellie to get dressed and they would all go to the theatre together. Don was at a loss as to what to do next. 'Do nothing,' Gertie advised. 'Leave her alone, she'll be all right.'

Nellie made her own way to the theatre and Don avoided speaking to her during band call. After her first show Don went to see her in her dressing room. Ever since Don had known Nellie he had done this and she always welcomed the quiet chat just between the two of them. On one occasion when Don had stopped off to speak to Ella Shields first, Nellie had marched into her dressing room and screamed at Don, 'Oh, there you are! You don't think to come to see me, do you?'

Liverpool was a triumphal success and on the back of this success the company were requested to perform many extra-mural activities such as opening bazaars, speaking at luncheons and teas, after theatre suppers, the list was endless. Don had to resist. Not only did he doubt the publicity value of such activities but it was unfair to ask his artistes to do extra work as well as their two nightly performances on stage. Although they were veterans, old timers, whatever, they would never make that an excuse for not participating in local events. Ella, George, Gertie, Billy and Talbot were angels and always ready to oblige if it had to be done. Don decided that all their energies had to be directed towards the stage performance primarily and if his artistes were not in tip-top condition they could not maintain their sparkling performances. It was often difficult to find adequate excuses for not being able to fulfil all the engagements requested of them.

Don saw to it that Nellie Wallace was never asked to perform any extra duties. Norah was sinking fast and needing more powerful sedation to dull her pain. This meant that on some occasions when Nellie spoke to her on the telephone Norah was unable to realise that it was her mother who was calling.

The inevitable happened. An urgent call from the hospital for Miss Wallace. Don and Gertie were ready to organise Nellie's travel arrangements but she would not accept any help. She asked the hotel reception to ring the station and book a sleeper for her to London. Remaining active, she saved herself from collapse.

A man standing at the reception desk recognised Nellie and offered to organise a sleeping berth for her, take her to the station in his car and see her safely on the train. He was a fan of Nellie, had heard of her plight and helped her at a time when she needed it most. As for Nellie, she found it easier to accept help from a total stranger.

Norah died on Thursday and was cremated on Saturday. Nellie re-joined the show the very next day in Sheffield.

When they opened in Glasgow the excitement was intense. The two weeks had already been sold out well ahead of the opening. As they arrived for the Monday morning band call the artistes could hardly get to the theatre for the queues of fans hoping for return tickets.

Harry Lauder visited them backstage after the second house opening night. When Don wanted to introduce him to the audience Harry refused. 'This is their night.' He pointed to the performers. 'I'm just one of the audience tonight. I always had a maxim. Please two-thirds of an audience and you're doing well. Nobody pleases everybody. But, this bunch! I'll wager there's not one person who is not completely carried away by each one of your artistes. There's George Elliott, bless him. Dear little Gertie, as fresh and lovely as ever. Nellie, Talbot and Randolph, and that wee Ella Shields. Why, man, I'd pay my money any night just to see her walk out on to the stage at the start of her act and then take her calls at the end. She's perfect, she is exquisite. I'd like to go backstage after the show to see the boys and girls.'

Harry went backstage and everyone greeted him singing his own songs. The electrician could not leave the theatre until the lights were switched off. Don took responsibility. The electrician went home, Harry kept on singing.

Their next venue was Edinburgh. They arrived at the Caledonian Hotel on Sunday ready to begin the following day. No sooner had they arrived than an official of the Scottish Homes Exhibition called on Don. He had agreed that the entire company should attend the opening at the Waverley Market the following day. It would mean good publicity for both sides but there was a problem. How were they all going to get there together and on time for the opening of the exhibition. Don promised that if the Scottish Homes Exhibition could provide the transport he would see to the rest.

Don and Gertie had invited the others to lunch with them at the Caledonian on the Monday so they would all be ready to set off from the same place for the exhibition. At 2.15 p.m. precisely the hotel porter informed Don, 'Mr Ross, your carriage awaits.'

As they gathered at the door of the hotel they were amazed to see an old open Landau complete with horses and liveried coachman. They had never expected quite such a grand mode of transport. As the carriage door was opened for them, Ella Shields hesitated. 'I'm all for showmanship but isn't this more like circus?'

'Get in the bloody thing,' Nellie Wallace reprimanded her with a sharp slap on the bottom. Everyone else piled in and Don sat on the box with the coachman. The front of the hotel was thronged with onlookers waiting to cheer them on their

*'Thanks for the Memory' performers leaving the Caledonian Hotel, Princes Street, Edinburgh.
From left, Gertie Gitana, Nellie Wallace, June Elliott, Don Ross, G.H. Elliott, Ella Shields*

way.

As the coach began to make its way along Princes Street, the mile-long route was lined with even more fans all shouting and waving. It was a terrific send-off as well as a wonderful welcome to the city of Edinburgh.

They trotted along at a sedate speed, feeling like Royalty. The coachman, Tom Vallance chatted to Don, 'Miss Gitana won't remember, but I drove her in my brougham every night when she worked at the Empire here thirty-five years ago.'

At the exhibition the artistes all made themselves available to photographers. Their first appointment was at the *Good Housekeeping* stand, opposite which was a stand promoting Harrogate Health Salts. The demonstrator was offering glasses of salts to passers-by to sample. A true cockney, he pushed glasses of the stuff into their hands, ''Ere you are then. 'Arrogate 'ealth salts. Look after yer insides and yer outside will look after itself.' He then noticed Nellie Wallace on the stand opposite. ''Ere, Nell, 'ave a swig.' Nellie raised her head and shot him a look of contempt. 'C'mon gel, 'ave a go. It's great for yer bowels.' Nellie turned to Don, 'Mr Ross, will you kindly inform that gentleman that Miss Wallace's bowels are in excellent working order.'

They moved on to their next photo session. Nellie still fuming, carried on a diatribe in her haughtiest manner. 'I don't know what the country's coming to. Here we are at this lovely exhibition, being treated like ladies and gentlemen and some upstart interrogates one about the condition of one's bowels! Presumption, my dear. They would never have asked Vesta Tilley about her bowels. But then, perhaps the poor bitch never had any.' Nellie was often heard to comment about music hall entertainers, 'We might be vulgar but we are not common.'

Edinburgh was as big a success as Liverpool and the people took them to their hearts. The Lord Provost invited the company to take tea with him at the City Chambers. In fact this became common practice. In each new town they appeared the Lord Mayor would entertain them and these occasions were always attended by the press.

It was during their Edinburgh appearance that Val Parnell telephoned Don, 'I'm taking you off the road and putting the show in for a season at the Prince of Wales Theatre here in London. Don replied, 'Oh no, Val, I wouldn't like that. We are music hall people and don't want to work theatres. The atmosphere is completely different.' Val was not impressed, as far as he was concerned it did not really matter what Don Ross might like. Don knew he was right and stuck to his guns. He had the most successful show that had been seen for years. It was his idea, his show and he would call the shots.

Don knew Val all too well. He could be difficult when he could not get his own way. He would use cajolery, flattery, threats, even blackmail if he thought it might serve his purpose but Don was on strong ground. Val was desperate to replace a poor show at the Prince of Wales and 'Thanks for the Memory' was the biggest thing in the country.

Val did resort to blackmail and threatened to cancel all the dates that Don had with Moss Empires for breach of contract. Don called his bluff, 'That's all right with me, Val, go ahead and cancel them. Prove to the world that you can cut off your nose and spite your face. We can survive. Nothing can stop us now. Been nice talking to you, Val. Goodbye.' Gertie had heard it all and agreed with Don's decision.

Val called again, and again but Don remained adamant: he would not, could not take his show off the road. They were playing to capacity houses as well as being fêted in every town and city they visited. There was nothing to gain and possibly everything to lose by acceding to Val's demands.

They continued their tour and it became customary for the press to visit their hotels for photo sessions. It was good, free publicity but inevitably the question of age was always raised. Whenever Don was asked to list their individual ages he replied, 'I wouldn't tell you even if I knew. If you think that is so important, why don't you ask them yourself? None of us are exactly young. We don't pretend to be young. I hope you don't expect to see antiques on display. You will see unadulterated music hall talent at its best. The likes of which you may never see again.' Don noted their cynicism as they smiled in a patronising fashion. However, after they had seen the show they would invariably seek out Don afterwards and comment, 'How right you were.' An unnecessary comment. He had always known that he was right.

The ageist attitude was prevalent in one Midland town when the Lord Mayor greeted them with the remark, 'Let us sit down and then you can tell me your ages.' Ella who, like everyone else, was becoming more than a little tired of this attitude, piped up, 'Oh what fun. Is this some new game? I suppose ages first, then first names after. Being Lord Mayor entitles you to have first go? What are you waiting for? Come on.' There was no further mention of ages.

After Edinburgh the show moved to Leeds and everyone became increasingly worried about Nellie. Quite apart from the fact that she was not eating she would spend longer periods alone in her dressing room, weeping. Naturally, she was grieving for her daughter but instead of progressing through the process Nellie seemed to become more morose as each day passed. It was always customary for music hall people to cling together and do what they could to support each other in times of crisis. When on tour with Don and Gertie it was more like being a part of one big caring family than a group of performers. Everyone wanted to comfort Nellie but it was almost impossible to get close to her. She insisted on keeping everyone at arm's length and everyone respected her wishes. She could not face anyone who might chatter to her. Nevertheless, she was made aware that all her colleagues were there if and whenever she might need them. Ella persuaded her to share her dressing room and promised to remain quiet. Nellie was surrounded by supportive, loving friends.

Despite her anguish Nellie never missed a single performance. She never failed to go on stage and make her audiences laugh and all the while she was crying, secretly, inside. The truth was that she did not dare accept help or sympathy from her colleagues for fear of breaking down completely.

It was Don who intervened. Nellie was torturing herself unnecessarily and he took it upon himself to call the theatre doctor. Don had expected a tirade from Nellie but she was suddenly acquiescent. After he examined Nellie the doctor confirmed that she was very ill. Although he could not give a specific diagnosis at that point, Don could. Nellie was dying of a broken heart.

The more Don tried to persuade Nellie to take time off the more she insisted on continuing. She pleaded with Don to let her work. He agreed on the condition that she should rest completely during the day until she was due on stage. There were to be no extra stints or charity work. Don was concerned about the lodgings she had in their next stop, Birmingham. Although Nellie insisted that they were first class, Don continued to worry. He knew she needed medical attention.

No sooner had Don and Gertie settled in their own accommodation in

Stourbridge when Randolph called. Nellie had left her rooms and was with him.

Don and Gertie collected Nellie from Randolph's place. They took her wrapped in a blanket, back to their own hotel and called a doctor. They had not expected good news. The doctor confirmed their worst fears, Nellie was desperately ill. Don had to be really firm with her and arranged for her return to her own home in London. She did not argue, Nellie was too ill to protest.

Val Parnell called Don again. 'I suppose you might condescend to work the London Palladium?' Don jumped at the chance. 'I would be honoured. That's our ground.'

'Right, you open on 5th July for two weeks. I've got a big star from America, Edgar Bergen, the ventriloquist, with Charlie McCarthy. They will feature in the first half of the show and I want just your seven stars for the second half. We have our own regular line of girls. How much is it going to cost us?'

Don had to think quickly. He knew to the nearest penny what his overheads were. He added a thousand pounds to that and gave Val a quote. 'Just what I reckoned myself,' a delighted Val replied. 'We'll call that a deal. I'll send you the contract right away.' Val's eager acceptance made Don wonder if he should have asked for more but he did not dwell on that for long. The Palladium was a first-class booking and he netted a profit of £2,000 which, in those days, was a great deal of money.

CHAPTER 10

THE PALLADIUM AND ONWARDS

As Val had promised, Don's company occupied the second half of the show. A spectacular finale had been designed. The entire stage was hung with black velvet. A long table set with crystal goblets and silver candelabra occupied centre stage. The glasses were filled with champagne for the artistes to drink a toast as the orchestra played 'Auld Lang Syne' and the movable platform rotated. It was an emotional end to a star-studded show and the audiences loved it so much that many returned several times to see the show again and again.

After their triumphal two weeks at the Palladium the next high spot was their appearance at that year's Royal Command Performance before King George VI and Queen Elizabeth, our present Queen Mother.

Nellie Wallace had recovered sufficiently to attend this illustrious occasion, which was to be her last stage appearance.

It was forbidden for anyone to wait in the wings during a Royal performance, they were kept in touch with events through an intercom system connected to each dressing room. As everyone awaited the arrival of Their Majesties, Don stood in the corridor and read the early edition of the *Evening Standard*. Maurice Wiggen's report on Don's artistes read thus:

Not merely nostalgia. The main reason for their success is the technical virtuosity of these stars. They come on and get straight to work with the confidence of mastery. It is this great quality of impact that these great artistes have. As English as apple pie, as rich as a round of roast beef, as stimulating as stout, they display the bold and generous vitality of an age

115

that was not afraid to laugh, and cry.

A resounding cheer from the audience signalled the arrival of the King and Queen and the show commenced. On the bill that night were Ted Ray and Julie Andrews, along with other well-known performers like Danny Kaye.

Nellie made the audience laugh as soon as she set foot on stage. She gave the performance of her life. As the curtain came down and Nellie left the stage she stumbled and Don caught her in his arms. Although she was exhausted, Nellie insisted on making the finale walk down.

Three weeks later Nellie died in a nursing home. A valve in her heart was torn, she had literally died of a 'broken heart'. *The Times* obituary read:

Nellie Wallace was in the royal line of Shakespeare's immortal clowns.

There could be no more fitting tribute to a truly great trouper.

Don and the rest of the company were surprised and shocked when they received Christmas cards from Nellie, each one written in her own hand. Randolph Sutton soon explained. Before her death Nellie had given him the cards which she had already addressed and stamped. 'I do not want to waste these lovely cards.'

Now Don had to find a replacement for Nellie. Lily Morris was the obvious choice and when Don approached her she agreed to 'give it a try'. Don arranged for her to join the show on 24th January 1949, when they opened at the Empire, Shepherd's Bush. Everyone sent flowers and went out of their way to make Lily feel welcome and part of the company. This was typical of music hall people, especially Don and Gertie. Everyone who worked with them were made to feel not merely valued colleagues, but a part of one large, happy family.

Lily was understandably nervous on her first night. She had not performed on stage for many years and Don and Gertie gave her all the support they could muster. This was also an opening night for Don and his usual fidgety nerves were apparent. The fact that Lily's husband insisted on singing 'Abide with Me' did not help matters.

Lily grabbed Don's hand on her way to the stage. 'Come with me, Billy boy, don't leave an old girl in the lurch.' Terrified of forgetting her lines, she begged Don to stand in the prompt corner, which he did for several performances until she regained her confidence. His presence was enough and Lily romped onto the stage like a two-year-old and revived her old songs, 'The Old Apple Tree' and 'Don't Have Any More, Mrs Moore'. She always ensured that she received more curtain calls than anyone else. As the applause began to subside Lily would rush back on the stage. Don was forced to remember that no-one could milk an audience quite like Lily.

Lily had been born Lilles Mary Crosbie and she was convinced that Bing Crosbie was a cousin of hers. When Gertie suggested that the only way to find out for certain was to contact Bing himself, Lily decided against such action. 'If he were related then I'd have to ask him to tea and that would mean an extra cup and saucer to wash-up. No. I really couldn't be bothered.'

'Thanks for the Memory' continued to fill theatres wherever it appeared and it was inevitable that Don should receive requests to take the show abroad. Offers came from agents in Australia, South Africa and Canada. Georgie Wood offered a tour of all the major American cities. They were all tempting propositions which Don felt bound to refuse. Wonderful performers as his artistes were, many of them were just not fit enough to even contemplate the exhausting schedules that such travel would entail. Randolph had a heart condition and Talbot, who was diabetic, was suffering from the early stages of gangrene. Don was not prepared to go anywhere with only half a company, so reluctantly but wisely he was forced to refuse a fabulous offer.

Shortly after this Lily suffered a stroke and was unable to work again.

Although every stage of the tour had proved to be an unmitigated success, their reception in Dublin was unprecedented. As usual all tickets had been sold well in advance of their arrival, queues surrounded the theatre hoping for returns or standing room. Don and Gertie were staying at the Gresham Hotel where they met film actor Victor Maclaglen. He was bemoaning the fact that it was impossible to get a ticket for 'Thanks for the Memory' at any price. Gertie offered to take him through the stage entrance with her that evening. Although he would not get a seat he would at least see the show. Standing at the back of the pit stalls Mr Maclaglen watched both performances that night and enjoyed it so much he returned every night during his stay in Dublin.

On the last night the queues of people trying to get in at all costs rushed the doors and forced their way into the auditorium. After the show none of the artistes could leave the theatre because of the crowds blocking the narrow alley where the stage door was situated. The dressing rooms overlooked this alley and the crowd called out to the artistes by name, requesting that they sing choruses of their individual songs. The crowds joined in with gusto.

This went on for some hours. Don had never experienced anything like it.

After Belfast they returned to London and a new home. Having lived in busy London for so long Don hankered for the wide open spaces of the countryside and room to stable a horse or two. On the outskirts of Elstree they found exactly what they were looking for. A spacious house with eleven acres of gardens including paddocks and a meadow. Beyond the orchard was a dear little cottage. The house was called Woodcock Hall but Don wanted to put his own stamp on the place so, taking the first and last syllables of the name of his show, he came up with Thanmory Court.

Gertie had not been enamoured with the idea of moving house at first but she was soon excited by the idea after seeing what she could do with Thanmory Court. A born home-maker she planned every step of their moving house down to the very last detail. The removals men knew in advance not only in which room to place each item of furniture but the exact spot in that room.

The cottage became Gertie's special project. It had four reasonably sized rooms plus a small kitchen. One of the rooms was converted into a bathroom, leaving two bedrooms and one good-sized living room. Don was perplexed by all this activity until Gertie explained that she had prepared the cottage for his mother and her companion, Talbollie, to move into. Gertie's mother-in-law was indeed delighted with the idea and wasted no time in giving up her own house in Leicester for her 'dream cottage'.

The show moved to Blackpool for the summer season and for the first time in its run Don felt that the audiences were not as enthusiastic as they might have been. For a start the Orchid Room was not a music hall but a venue which was more accustomed to seeing sophisticated night club audiences. A managerial mistake possibly but it made Don take stock. Perhaps his show had run its course. Both he and Gertie made the decision to book their final appearances for the week commencing 27th November at the Empress, Brixton. They would finish where they had started.

Don had to face a deal of argument about his decision. The artistes themselves agreed that it was better to leave their audiences wanting. Many theatre managers requested just one more date. Many venues they had not yet played begged Don to think again before taking the show off the road. Others accused him of having lost his sanity to remove such a money spinner but Don remained adamant. After all, when he had first envisaged the idea of such a show he had expected it to run for a year at the most. It was now 1950, the show had been on the road for almost three years.

When they were in Norwich, honouring one of their remaining dates, Don's secretary telephoned from London to say that *The People* newspaper had asked for copies of photographs of the artistes appearing in 'Thanks for the Memory'. They wanted to print a feature article about them. Don agreed to the release of the photographs.

As they were preparing to leave their hotel on the Sunday Don read the report in *The People*. It was the cruellest piece of journalism that he had ever seen. Not wishing to upset Gertie he said nothing but he should have known that it was impossible to fool Gertie. She sensed that something was not right and insisted on finding the cause. When Don gave her the gist of the scandalous report in *The People* she gave her usual support, 'Now look, darling, we've been travelling round the country for three years and everyone has been wonderful to us. Theatres have been packed. Four weeks in Glasgow, six in Manchester, five in Liverpool and just think what Dublin was like. Why upset yourself about some little upstart who chooses to write disparagingly about us? He's not the voice of the people, he's just a miserable undersized extrovert trying to attract attention to himself by saying the opposite to what everyone else has said.'

Although Gertie displayed good commonsense as always, she could not dispel Don's air of gloom. It was made worse as soon as they reached home and Belle told them of the endless stream of calls that had been coming in about the scurrilous article. Many friends were advising that Don should contact his solicitors immediately.

Blanche Robey telephoned. What they had to say about George was disgraceful. They had shown a picture of him drinking a glass of champagne to celebrate his eightieth birthday and said that they would have preferred to see him drinking to his final stage appearance. Whatever Don decided to do Blanche would contact her solicitors first thing next morning.

They were due to open at the Palace Theatre, Ramsgate, the following night. When Don and Gertie arrived the entire company was up in arms about the article. Some spoke of taking legal advice. Ella Shields disagreed. 'My dears, I wouldn't lower my dignity to let the man even know that I read his article.' Don did take legal advice but eventually it was decided by all not to take any action. In fact, the writer of that article had unwittingly done them all a great favour. Audiences were even warmer and more demonstrative toward them for the remainder of the run.

It had to come. The final week of 'Thanks for the Memory' arrived. Don was inundated with requests for last-minute tickets. People were prepared to pay anything and those who had never queued in their lives were waiting outside the Brixton Empress for returns or unreserved seats, they would accept standing room, anything for a chance to see the last show. As well as being the final week of 'Thanks for the Memory', it would also be Gertie's final farewell to the stage.

When Don and Gertie arrived at the theatre for that last performance there was already a mountain of telegrams in their dressing room. One was from their Majesties the King and Queen and Don went to each dressing room before the show began to show each artiste the message. There was one from Marius Goring, 'Thanks, not only for the memory but for showing my generation how it should be done.'

The bouquets, boxes of chocolates and other gifts were arriving so quickly that the stage door keeper could not cope. Don had to organise a chain of stage hands to pass the items from the door into the theatre under the stage, where he sorted them into sections pertaining to each artiste. The flow was continuous and it meant that Don was kept so busy he was unable to watch the final performance of his show. He could hear the applause as each artiste made their entrance and after they had finished. Even below stage the warmth and affection that emanated from that audience was palpable.

As each artiste took their final call Don arranged for the tributes to be handed onto the stage. There were so many they took up most of the stage area. With more than three hundred tributes for Gertie alone, there was hardly room for the performers to take their final bows. The applause continued, ovation followed upon ovation, the audience would not let them go.

Don was presented with a magnificent silver salver engraved with the signatures of everyone who had participated in the show, as well as a silver ash tray. Ella Shields gave him an inscribed silver tankard.

*** *** ***

And suddenly, that was it. The time that no-one had wanted to see, although they all knew it had to come. Final speeches were made and Gertie bade farewell to her last audience. They did the best they could to join hands for 'Auld Lang Syne' before the final curtain fell on 'Thanks for the Memory' at the Brixton Empress on 2nd December 1950.

There had been so much emotional energy expended on that last night that, when it was time to close, everyone involved was so utterly exhausted they simply went quietly to their dressing rooms. Not one word was spoken, no tear was shed. There was only silence.

The following night Gertie and Don invited everyone to a party at 'Thanmory Court'.

Finale at the Palladium.
From left, Randolph Sutton (Ran), Gertie Gitana, Ella Shields, Talbot O'Farrell, Nellie Wallace, Billy Danvers and G.H. Elliott.

CHAPTER 11

THE FINAL CURTAIN

After retiring Gertie had time to follow her own interests. She developed a keen interest in the stock market. It was said that she never got out of bed before reading the *Financial Times*. As she sipped her morning tea she would go through the share index, showing an almost childish delight whenever her investments were doing well. Gertie was a shrewd investor and would also advise Don on such matters. So successful was she at judging the best buys that Don christened her 'Golden Fingers'.

Certainly Gertie enjoyed her little gambles on the stock market. It was exciting and rewarding but the accumulation of money was not the reason for her interest. Gertie had never been one to hanker after money for its own sake, probably because she had never had to worry about it.

Throughout her life Gertie had enjoyed financial security, consequently she was always ready to help any friend in financial need or even a stranger. This giving was always done quietly and without ceremony. She gave unstintingly to charity and never ignored a begging letter.

Gertie was not alone in this. Music hall people were notorious for their generosity, especially to colleagues down on their luck. Most performers came from working class families and had known hardship before success, and many had to take on family responsibilities down to the fourth generation once they started earning the big money. This is why many great names died leaving estates that seemed small and hardly commensurate with the kind of money they had earned during a brilliant career. Much of the money had been given away.

Don and Gertie were no different and until the end of her life Gertie would send money every Friday to what she called her 'pensioners'. Don would personally buy the registered envelopes on his way home from the office. They were sent to people whom Gertie had known and had fallen on hard times. An old lady who used to be one of her dressers, a landlady who had been especially kind, a young boy stricken by a paralysing illness, as well as members of her own family and friends. After Gertie's death there were still seven surviving 'pensioners'. Don continued to see that they were paid as before because that is what she would have wanted.

A day at the races became a regular treat. There had been little time for such frivolity when working and two shows a night demanded every available ounce of energy. Don would take a day off from his office and he and Gertie enjoyed that precious time together. They would often cross over to Ireland to attend the Punchestown races and the Naas Hunt Ball.

Fridays were special. Don always reserved this time to lunch with Gertie at Kettner's in Soho and after lunch she would wander through the street markets and colourful shops; a born collector, she had an eye for a bargain and invariably went home with some piece of antique china which she had managed to secure for a good price.

Gertie was also a homemaker but she had never had time for it during her working life; now, in retirement, she could indulge herself. She enjoyed gardening, needlework and all the little mundane household chores became labours of love. Don would often have to call to her to come indoors when it was almost too dark to see, but there was always just a bit more to be done before calling it a day.

Like most music hall folk, Don, Gertie and Belle enjoyed a game of cards. It was a way of entertaining themselves and enjoying the company of colleagues whilst they were touring. After a show it was customary for a group of like-minded friends to meet and relax over a game of cards. Don had always looked forward to these sessions when, after a long day's work, the three would play cards after dinner. He counted those evenings among his happiest and cursed the invention of the television, which meant that card playing evenings became fewer and far between.

Gertie was undoubtedly a rich woman and could afford to live in style but apart from a cook, a maid and a chauffeur, because neither Don nor Gertie ever learned to drive, she lived quite modestly. Certainly she lived in beautiful houses furnished with impeccable taste and she could afford to wear mink, but neither she or Don ever went in for entertaining on a grand scale. People were not encouraged to 'drop in' uninvited. A few close friends, such as Ted Ray and his wife, Sybil, George and June Elliott would often be invited for Sunday lunch but there were never any grand parties. Gertie would have considered that to be far too ostentatious.

Don continued with his business activities and it often meant his working long hours and frequenting bars and clubs in order to discuss business with artistes and other agents. Gertie did not drink, and hanging around in smoke-filled clubs exchanging gossip had never appealed to her, so she was quite happy to let Don deal with those occasions alone. Whenever Gertie did accompany Don and other music hall artistes were present, she was constantly badgered into giving a chorus or two of Nellie Dean. Although she hated it whenever she was cornered in such a manner, Gertie would always respond with her usual good-natured charm.

Gertie would, however, always play an active part in all Don's productions. He never did get over his 'first night nerves' and it was always Gertie who sat out front on the opening nights. She never missed a rehearsal or the opportunity to correct anything which appeared to her to be less than perfect.

There was one occasion, however, when she was unable to offer advice. As a member of the audience at the Palladium Gertie was seen to wince as one of the 'stars' muffed an entrance, totally dependent on the microphone which she tried unsuccessfully to conceal in a bouquet of flowers. This notable performance was completed when the star of the show almost fell down the steps in the walk down at the end of the show.

Don and Gertie were enjoying a quiet day together with Georgie Wood when the telephone rang. They were expecting Ella Shields to call to say what time she would be joining them the following day but instead of Ella's voice on the other end of the line a stranger delivered the sad news that Miss Shields had collapsed after her performance. They had found a card in her handbag stating that, in the event of such an emergency, Miss Gitana should be notified.

Ella never regained consciousness and she died two days later.

One afternoon another surprise telephone call brought exciting news. Percy Hughes, manager of the Theatre Royal, Hanley, spoke to Don: I want to be the first to tell you that the City Council have just decided to rename Frederick Street and call it Gitana Street in honour of Gertie.'

Gertie was indeed honoured and moved by this gesture. She considered it to be greatest tribute that anyone could desire, to be remembered and rewarded by the people of her own home town. Just as she had been remembered when 'Thanks for the Memory' played at Hanley and the entire population of the town turned out to greet their arrival.

After Don and Gertie had lived at Thanmory Court for five years they decided to move again. Although they loved the house and its location, it was becoming a chore to have to travel daily to the West End for business and entertainment and their friends who had no transport of their own had difficulty visiting unless Don sent a car for them. They decided on a house in Haverstock Hill, Hampstead.

Gitana Street, Hanley

Belle was delighted with it. 'You can keep your damn fields. This is better.' Don and Gertie did not argue, they were townsfolk after all. They named their new house 'Neldean'.

It was a big job, preparing to move from Thanmory. Gertie had collected a great deal over the years and she personally supervised the packing up. During her many visits to Ireland she had always returned with fresh supplies of the beautiful linen. Her monogram was embroidered on every item. Gertie would not allow her maid to remove the linens from the well-stocked cupboard, insisting on climbing the step ladder herself to reach the top shelf. At the top of the ladder she turned the wrong way, overbalanced and fell 'with a terrible crash' as her maid later told Don.

It had indeed been a bad fall, Gertie was knocked out for a short time. Typically, she brushed the matter aside and insisted that Don should not hear of it, she would be perfectly all right after a little rest.

It was several months later when Don noticed that Gertie seemed to be in pain, although she said nothing. 'What is it, darling?'

Gertie made light of it, 'It's nothing, just a little nagging pain below the armpit. I've had it a week or two, on and off.'

'I know all about your fall. I think you should have an X-ray.'

Gertie embraced her husband. 'Poor old Bill. You're always worrying about me. You know I've never been ill in my life. Stop worrying.'

Nothing more was said until some weeks later when they went to Broadstairs for a short holiday. As they walked along the jetty in the warm June sunshine Gertie suddenly winced and held her side. She was obviously in pain and Don insisted that they return home immediately to seek medical advice.

Gertie was examined by a doctor, a specialist and had X-rays taken. There was nothing abnormal that could be detected, she was given the all clear. As they left the consulting rooms in Harley Street Don and Gertie skipped down the stairs like a couple of children, so delighted and relieved were they to hear the good news.

Their happiness was to be short-lived. The gnawing pain returned and persisted. Don insisted that Gertie should return to their doctor for advice. He decided that Gertie should undergo a series of tests at St John and Elizabeth hospital. Don visited every day and at the end of two weeks the specialist informed Don and Gertie that he would need to perform an exploratory operation to ascertain the exact cause of the trouble.

Don hoped that Gertie had not noticed the involuntary tightening of his hand on her shoulder as the consultant's words came home to him. Neither he nor Gertie said a word. There was nothing to say or do but await the results of the investigations.

Don was allowed to visit his wife after the operation. She was lying still and quiet in the bed as Don tiptoed quietly to her side. Gertie opened her eyes, 'My Bill,' she smiled. 'Have they said anything yet? It's nothing malignant, is it, Bill? They'd tell you if it were, wouldn't they?'

Don knelt by the bedside so that he could place his head beside hers on the pillow. They held hands in silence.

Later, the surgeon entered the room and asked to speak to Don. Gertie looked from one to the other anxiously and was reassured by her surgeon. 'There is nothing malignant.'

If Don had begun to believe those words his hopes were soon to be cruelly dashed. 'Mr Ross, one of the most difficult things a doctor has to do is to tell a man he is going to lose his wife.'

Don could not believe his own hearing as the voice continued, 'I'm sorry to tell you there is nothing we can do. If only we had got to her even three months ago, there might have been a chance, but now, it's too late. The cancer has invaded the liver . . .'

Grasping at straws, Don heard himself saying, 'We have money. Is there someone in the world, somewhere, who might be able . . . We would pay anything, anything at all.'

The surgeon was adamant. 'Nothing can be done.'

'How long?'

'Six months at the most.'

Don was left in the corridor, alone and bewildered. He forced himself to return to Gertie. She would worry if he was away too long and yet he did not know how he was going to face her. How to keep up the pretence with a brave face while his heart was breaking?

Gertie was concerned when Don returned to her room, shooting questions at him. 'You wouldn't lie to me, would you, Bill?'

Don had to perform the greatest acting role of his life as he consoled her, 'I wouldn't lie to you, darling. You know that.'

He did not want to leave her but, afraid to stay, he was saved by a nurse who suggested that Mrs Ross needed to rest. Don kissed Gertie before walking out of the hospital into the night. As he walked the doctor's words repeated themselves in his mind. 'Nothing can be done,' 'Six months at the most.'

Unable to face Belle, Don went into a public house and sat in a quiet corner with a drink. He sat there until he felt a touch on his sleeve. He was informed by the barmaid that it was now closing time. He had been sitting in the corner for hours as silent tears streamed down his face. He walked home.

Belle started to castigate him for being late until she saw the agony in his face. 'What is it, Bill?'

'Cancer. Six months.' It was all he could say.

Belle, refusing to accept the news, turned her anger on Don. 'That's a lie. Gertie has never been ill in her life. How dare you come home and tell me such stuff.' Unable to take any more he pushed her gently away from him into an armchair and slumped on the floor beside her. They held hands and sobbed out their grief.

Daily bulletins appeared in all major newspapers giving news of Gertie's progress after her operation. Floral tributes from her many fans were arriving daily but one special tribute came via the telephone. George Elliott spoke to Gertie from Newcastle.

I had to call you, Darling. Last night I was called to the stage door to see a man who said he had a party of forty Gertie Gitana fans who were going to the second house. They had heard of your illness and asked if we, as a message of affection, would sing 'Nellie Dean' at the finale of the show. So we all lined up, Hetty, Dorothy Ward, Shaun Glenville, Billy Danvers, myself and all the other acts in the show. We started to sing 'Nellie Dean' and the whole audience rose to their feet and sang like a choir. I've never heard anything so lovely and moving. I simply had to telephone and tell you all about it.

Once Gertie had recovered from the operation Don was advised to take her home. There was little point in her remaining in hospital when there was no treatment available for her. She would be happier in her own surroundings. Gertie had struck up a relationship with an Irish nurse called Winnie and it was arranged that she should continue to care for Gertie in her own home.

When Gertie returned to Haverstock Hill she was met by a fantastic array of flowers in the hall. A huge basket from Dorothy Ward said quite simply, 'Welcome Home'.

Surrounded by her own familiar possessions in her own home Gertie thrived. Before long she was able to take a taxi to Hampstead Heath with her nurse and enjoy a walk in the fresh air. She was even able to resume her regular luncheon dates with Don in the West End at Kettners on a Friday. As long as she rested and took life at an easy pace, she was able to cope with her usual daily activities. Don began to hope against hope that the doctors might be wrong in their prognosis.

Eventually, inevitably she began to tire and outings became too arduous to contemplate. It soon became too much of an effort to venture downstairs. Gertie spent more time in her bedroom.

On Christmas Eve the local Salvation Army Band paid a visit. Gertie had always supported the 'Sallyann' and they asked if she would like them to sing for her. She requested that they sing 'Adeste Fideles', 'Once in Royal David's City' and 'Silent Night'. The choir crowded into the hall and Gertie made her way downstairs to listen. For the first and last time she sat on the settee that was Don's Christmas present to her. Gertie had admired that particular piece of furniture in Maples store and Don had arranged for it to be delivered as a Christmas surprise.

Although she had been able to summon the strength to walk down the stairs, Don had to carry her back to her room.

It was soon after Christmas that Winnie approached Don. He must prepare himself for his wife's impending death. The nurse was sure that Gertie could not last another week. Don, of course, refused to believe it. Gertie looked so well, she had roses in her cheeks and he knew she suffered no pain, thank God for that.

Certainly, she tired easily, so what. She was nothing like a dying woman as far as he was concerned. It could not be true.

Don crept up the stairs to Gertie's room. The door was slightly ajar, he could hear her whispering, 'Holy Mary, Mother of God. In the hour of death be with me.' He was to hear this simple prayer again and again whenever Gertie thought she was alone.

Eventually, Don had to accept that the last hours of Gertie's life were slipping away. They both knew it and yet pretended not to know. Not wishing to set up a bedside vigil Don continued with his usual daily routine of leaving the house for the office. One Thursday morning a telephone call from Winnie to say that Gertie was asking for him brought Don rushing home. Expecting the worst, he grabbed the first available taxi.

Gertie was sitting by the fire in her room, 'Darling, you didn't mind having Winnie telephone, did you? I just felt I wanted you here with me.' It was all too clear that time was short and Don remained by his wife's side until the end.

On Saturday morning Don was sitting with Gertie, talking of this and that, when she suddenly said, 'Fancy them naming that street in Hanley after me.' Don placed his head on her pillow, his face close to hers,

Somehow, she managed to find the strength to put her hand at the back of my neck and press my face closer to hers. She held it there for a time and whispered, 'Thank you, Bill, for all your kindness, all your goodness to me, dear, and for all your love. Don't try to live with me when I have gone. No-one should ever live with the dead. Be happy, darling.' Gradually her hand relaxed, her eyes closed.

When the end came it was peaceful. Don took his beloved Gertie in his arms and kissed her goodbye.

George and June Elliott came to offer what comfort they could. Neighbours also paid their respects and talked in subdued tones around Don, who sat silently trying to come to terms with the fact that his Darling was dead. They stayed until the early hours, then, slowly, silently, one by one they took their leave.

'Go to bed, darling,' Belle advised.

'You go. I'll come later.'

As Don heard the clock strike five that morning in a suddenly cold and empty house he slowly dragged himself up the stairs, like an old man. He told himself, 'The worst thing that could ever happen to you has happened. Nothing else will ever hurt you quite as much.' As painful as that thought was, it was also strangely comforting.

Don was surrounded by kind, caring friends as well as the usual press intrusion and thoughtless folk who called at the house to ask for a memento of Gertie. It served to keep him occupied and prevented, for a while at least, the pain which would inevitably ensue. That evening Don and Belle watched the news on television announcing Gertie's death.

Telegrams and letters of sympathy poured in, thousands of them, and Don answered every single one. It had always been a rule of Gertie's that all correspondence should be answered personally and promptly.

W. Macqueen Pope paid tribute to Gertie's life and career in a radio broadcast which Don and Belle listened to a little reluctantly, but Don said later,

Popie's lovely tribute and hearing Gertie's own voice singing many of her famous songs made me feel proud that such a wonderful person had been my wife. I cried tears of sadness and joy all the way through.

After a service at Brompton Oratory the coffin was taken by train to Leicester where it rested overnight in St Mary's Roman Catholic church. The following day, 'under a dark and threatening sky' Gertie was laid to rest in Wigston cemetery on 12th January 1957. Masses of floral tributes had been fastened to the railings of the cemetery by her fans.

Don sought permission from Wigston Urban Council for a verse of 'Nellie Dean' to be inscribed on a headstone for the grave. Although they thought it a little unusual, permission was duly granted.

Every major newspaper in the land eulogised Gertie Gitana.

Clarkson Rose, in his book, *Red Plush and Greasepaint*, stated,

There has been no greater idol of the halls than Gertie Gitana. No artiste

Don and Gertie's headstone in the cemetery at Wigston Magna

has ever belonged more to the music hall than Gertie. She was universally loved by the stalls, the gallery and the pit of whatever hall she appeared in. She mesmerised all and sundry with her simplicity of approach and obvious sincerity. Men wished that they were the one who sat and dreamed by the old mill stream with her.

One of her closest friends, Ted Ray said of her,

She was the most gentle, lovable person I have ever met. Gertie was a real star. The right kind of star. A perfect artiste in every sense of the word. I place her among the immortals.

Not one person who had ever known Gertie could dispute that. She was music hall at its very best. She had known fame and fortune and remained unspoilt. She was always the same generous-hearted woman whom many were proud to call friend. She gave unstintingly to charity but, apart from having a street in Hanley named after her, she never received the public recognition which she so richly deserved. Gertie Gitana never appeared in an Honours List. But then, she might have considered such a tribute to be too grand for one who was known as 'The Idol of the People'.

During the 1959 Edinburgh Festival Gertie's Scottish fans arranged for a memorial seat to be placed in Princes Street with a plaque bearing the inscription:

A LOVING REMEMBRANCE OF
GERTIE GITANA
MUSIC HALL ARTISTE
'There's an old mill by the stream,
Nelly Dean.'

Don beside Gertie's portrait in the Gertie Gitana Room at the former Gaiety Theatre, South Wigston
(Reproduced by kind permission of The Leicester Mercury*)*

A pause during a senti-
mental journey for Mr Don
Ross, who is touring Scot-
land with a bus party from
London. Husband of the
former music hall artist,
Gertie Gitana, he is seen
on the seat in Princes
Street, Edinburgh, which
was dedicated to her
memory seven years ago by
a group of admirers. This
is Mr Ross' first visit to
Edinburgh since his wife's
death. Below—the plaque
on the seat names the song
made popular by Miss
Gitana, who appeared in
Edinburgh on many occa-
sions at the Empire and
Theatre Royal. Her last
appearance here was in
1948, in a bill which starred
veteran music hall artists.

Don in Princes Street, Edinburgh
(Reproduced by kind permission of The Edinburgh Evening News*)*

AFTERMATH

A fter Gertie's death Don almost became a recluse. Dorothy Ward offered to come out of retirement if he would agree to write and stage another pantomime, *Dick Whittington*. When she took a pair of scissors and ceremoniously cut his black tie it gave him the kick start that he needed to begin living again.

In 1963, along with Ray Mackender and Gerry Glover, Don was responsible for the founding of the British Music Hall Society. The title was Don's idea and he was their first Chairman. Some years later, in 1978, he was awarded the honour of King Rat.

Don Ross was a self-made man who enjoyed many successes in his long career. He always maintained that 'Thanks for the Memory' was his greatest achievement and certainly the one for which he would wish to be remembered.

He is properly remembered as a gentleman. A gentleman of the music hall whose word was his bond.

Don Ross died on 6th February 1980, ten weeks after suffering a stroke. He was laid to rest beside his beloved Gertie in Wigston cemetery after a service at the Actors' Church, Covent Garden. The Poet Laureate, Sir John Betjeman, read the lesson.

The final words belong to Don.

It seems so long since I heard the call that rang through the corridors of hundreds of music halls, 'The act that you follow is on their finish.' Then the call-boy's voice, 'All down for the finale, please.'
So this is the end of the show.

Don, taken shortly before his death

There is a bustle on the stairs leading down to the stage. We assemble. Someone is saying, 'We'll have to spread out. There are not many of us left.'

***   ***   ***

Not Heav'n itself upon the past has pow'r,
But what has been, has been, and I have had my hour.
Dryden

Dedication to Don in St. Paul's Church, Covent Garden